I SAW GOD

The True Story of a Young Boy's Miraculous Return from Death

James Anderson

SERAPHINA PRESS

Seraphina Press
212 3rd Avenue North, Suite 290
Minneapolis, MN 55401
612.455.2293
www.SeraphinaPress.com

ISBN-13: 978-0-9848028-0-7
LCCN: 2011943778

Distributed by Itasca Books

Cover Design by Scott Sword

Typeset by Wendy Arakawa

Author Website: www.ISawGodBooks.com
Printed in the United States of America

SERAPHINA
PRESS

I SAW GOD

*The True Story of a Young Boy's
Miraculous Return from Death*

*This book is dedicated
to the most remarkable woman I know—my mother,
Dorothy Anderson,
whose courage, strength, and cheerfulness
in the face of life's trials
still fills me with awe.*

Table of Contents

Acknowledgements

THIS WAS NEVER MEANT to be a book. When I began to write this story, my only intent was to capture this miraculous event on paper before it was lost in time. I thought it would be no more than eight or ten pages and would only circulate within the Anderson family. However, the story quickly assumed a life of its own and grew into a full-length narrative. It almost seemed to write itself.

Friends and relatives I shared it with fell in love with the story and urged me to explore the possibility of getting it published as a book. At first I balked at the idea. Then a dear friend reminded me that we are both the recipients *and* the stewards of God's miracles and that sharing this story would bless and inspire people around the world and bring glory to His name. She said it was a story "that begs to be told." Though I'd never thought of myself as an author, I couldn't argue with that and…well, here we are.

But this is certainly not the work of one man. No project like this could have been completed without the help and assistance of many other people. That being true, I'd like to gratefully acknowledge those who contributed their time and talent to the research, writing, and editing of this book.

First of all, I'd like to thank the many family members who provided me with innumerable details of the accident and its aftermath. My own recollections and the contributions of family members truly brought the story to life. My sincerest thanks go to my mother, Dorothy Anderson; my uncle, David Anderson; my aunt, Pat Anderson; and my siblings, Diana, Kathy, Bob, John, and of course, Bill.

I would also like to express my appreciation to Dr. James Gifford and Brett Nance of the Jesse Stuart Foundation for their support and encouragement during the writing of this book, as well as the JSF Reading Circle, and John Cannon of *The Daily Independent*, for their wonderful suggestions to help refine and expand various aspects of the story.

In the medical community, I'd like to thank Larry Ball and Teresa Nunley of Cabell Huntington Hospital and Erma Abbott of Tri-State Neurosurgical Consultants Inc., for their time and assistance in locating medical records; and Kathy Johnson, David Shiels, and Thelma Nicely of St. Mary's Hospital for providing background and biographical information on Dr. Thomas J. Holbrook.

Special thanks are due to Tom Carver, Jr., for his honesty, candor, and kindness during our discussion on the accident; to Melissa Reed Trent, a former neighbor who supplied key details about the accident; and to Dr. and

ACKNOWLEDGEMENTS

Mrs. John Holbrook, MD, and the family of Thomas J. Holbrook, for their much-welcomed support and cooperation.

Finally, I'd like to recognize the efforts of a wonderful group of personal friends for their gentle critique of the manuscript itself. My heart-felt thanks to Jolinda Kimbrell Conley, Susan Fleming, Kathy Lother, Connie Griffith Sloan, Sonya O'Brien, Greg Hammond, Lynne-Reed Carter, and Sherri Nibert Davis. Your encouragement and insightful comments were truly invaluable.

To God be the Glory!

Jim Anderson

November, 2010

Preface

ASHLAND—A five-year-old Ashland boy, riding a tricycle near his home in the 2700 block of Monroe Street, was seriously injured at 4:53 PM Thursday, when he was struck by a car. Billy Anderson, son of Mr. and Mrs. James Anderson…was in critical condition today at Cabell-Huntington Hospital where he underwent brain surgery after the accident. His brother, Jimmy, 12, also struck by the vehicle, driven by Thomas P. Carver II… was treated in King's Daughters Hospital emergency room for a leg injury and released…

So began a front-page story in the *Ashland Daily Independent* detailing the events of Thursday, February 26, 1970, the day a horrifying traffic accident briefly took the life of my five-year-old brother Billy. That my brother departed this life, however briefly, is central to the story. To quote Dickens, "This must be distinctly understood, or nothing wonderful will come of the story I'm going to relate." Unlike the novels of Dickens, however, this is not a work of fiction. It is a true story.

Little Billy, whose head was literally crushed by the front bumper of a speeding car, died three times prior to emergency surgery and was left in a vegetative coma after large portions of his damaged brain were removed. Although given no hope to live by his doctors, God had other plans— healing Billy in a stunning display of miracle-working power, turning family tragedy into unexpected triumph. Yet beyond the undeniably miraculous healing, little Billy Anderson was granted a glimpse of Heaven and returned with a message that Jesus will soon be coming back to the Earth.

Unfortunately, following his recovery, Billy lost all recollection of his visits to Heaven, leaving him with a gnawing life-long hunger to know what happened to him during his Near-Death Experience. Yet the story doesn't end here.

Forty years after the accident, in a dramatic session with a clinical psychologist, the memories of his remarkable out-of-body encounters, including his conversations with Jesus, were completely restored. During an extraordinary 90-minute hypnotherapy session, Bill re-lived the entire ordeal, describing exactly what happened to him in the hours after the accident.

The last chapter of this book includes a gripping question-and-answer session with Bill, covering all aspects of his Near-Death Experience in startling detail. Now, through Bill's eyes, we have the blessed opportunity to learn what it's like to venture beyond the veil and into Heaven itself, to experience the electrifying presence of the Son of God, and to return to Earth again.

I've had the privilege of sharing this story with personal friends many times through the years, and I am again privileged to share it with you. It is an incredible story of God's mercy and grace, a heartbreaking and heartwarming story you will long remember...a story that begs to be told.

That I may publish with the voice of thanksgiving,
and tell of all thy wondrous works.
—Psalms 26:7 (KJV)

1

A Little Adventure

April 5, 2010

YOU COULDN'T HAVE ORDERED a prettier day out of a catalog. Bright and sunny, with temperatures in the low seventies, it was picture-perfect for early April. If it weren't for the bare trees that lined each side of I-77, you'd have sworn it was June.

"Nervous?" I asked, as Bill and I snaked our way northward toward Parkersburg, West Virginia.

"No. I'm surprisingly calm. I'm more excited than nervous," Bill replied. "It's like going on a little adventure."

I readily agreed, "Yeah, that's a good way to describe it—'a little adventure'. You could also call it 'a little gamble'. Don't forget—there's definitely some risk involved, you know."

"Well, if it's a gamble, it's one I'm very willing to take. You just don't know what it's been like living with a…a hole in your life."

That caught my attention.

"A hole in your life?" I repeated. "What in the world does that mean?"

Turning his head and gazing out the window at the passing scenery, I could see that Bill was struggling to find words to describe what he was feeling. After a long minute, he continued, "It's really hard to explain. It's like you've lost a huge piece of your life and you don't have a clue what that piece is, or how it got misplaced, or why it's even important. You just know it's missing."

I'd never heard my brother talk like that before and I found it a little unsettling. Although we'd discussed *The Accident* countless times over the last forty years, Bill never let on that it troubled him in any significant way. In fact, Bill didn't usually have much to say about it whenever the subject came up. He knew the details from what he'd been told, but all he really knew about it was...well, what he'd been told. After all, he was only five years old when it happened and he didn't have any real memories of the incident, so no one in the family thought it affected his life that much as an adult.

"You mean, you feel like these missing memories have left a void in your life that you'd prefer not to have?" I asked.

"Yes," Bill answered, after a few seconds of reflection.

"I'd think just the opposite would be true—that you'd be glad *not* to have any memories of the accident at all, as bad as it was."

"I told you it was hard to explain. All I can say is that when you can't remember *anything* about the single most important event—good or bad—that ever happened in your life, it somehow eats away at you. At least it does me. It might have been bad, but it was still a part of my life—a huge part. Not remembering anything about it just fills me with questions…and those questions haunt me all the time."

"Really?" I replied, surprised. "I had no idea."

"I tell you, Jim, it's always been in the back of my mind, and somehow I just *feel* it. I'd give anything to able to remember something—anything—about it. Everyone tells me I died and went to Heaven, that I saw God and God healed me, but I have *no memory* of that whatsoever. Tell me that wouldn't affect you."

Suddenly, I began to see my brother in a very different light.

I knew all about the physical damage the accident had caused, but I'd never given any thought to the toll it may have taken on his psyche. Bill always seemed like a normal, well-adjusted adult. I never imagined that the accident spawned some vague psychological pressure that hounded him through the years and was evidently growing more intense as he got older.

As the miles flew by, a realization dawned on me.

"So that's why you were so insistent on finding a hypnotherapist?" I asked.

"Yes," Bill admitted with a gentle nod of his head.

"I had to see if there was some way to fill in the 'hole'...before it swallowed me up...completely."

Now it all made sense.

When Bill asked me a few months ago if I would help him find a qualified hypnotherapist—someone who might be able to help recover his "lost" memories of Heaven—I eagerly jumped at the chance. I'd always wanted to find out more about his after-life experiences too. Although his insistence struck me as a bit odd at the time, I never realized it was a cry for help. I had no idea that the man I'd known for forty-five years was struggling against a gnawing obsession he was powerless to satisfy, and losing ground all the time.

"Well, Bill, I won't pretend to know what you've been living with. I just hope we've found an answer to whatever is troubling you."

Wanting to brighten the mood in the car, Bill replied with a smile, "Don't worry, brother. I'll be all right. I'm just thrilled to know there's something that might end this torment and give me some peace of mind."

I felt a sudden big-brotherly urge to remind Bill of the dangers involved.

"I have to admit—I admire your courage. If it was me, I think I'd leave it alone. As I've said before, you might uncover something you'll regret knowing later on. Maybe there's a good reason why you've never been able to recall your out-of-body experience."

"Maybe...but I'm willing to take the chance."

Feeling I should press the point one more time, I added, "Remember what Stephanie said—you might get more than you bargained for. There's a good chance we won't recover any memories at all and, if we do, they might not be as satisfying or pleasant as you think."

Bill's confidence never waivered, "Yes, I remember what she said. In any event, it's too late to back out now. We're almost there."

'Stephanie' was Stephanie Phelps, a Certified Advanced Clinical Hypnotherapist who worked at The Counseling House in Parkersburg—our destination that day. After three months of searching, I'd finally found a therapist both Bill and I felt comfortable with. Stephanie and I had exchanged a number of emails over the last few weeks and had spent a considerable amount of time on the phone discussing Bill's case. In my quest to find the right clinician for our "little adventure" Stephanie seemed to fit the bill exactly, no pun intended.

She came highly recommended, and on top of it all, she herself had had an out-of-body experience following a truck wreck some years before. Exploring a near-death occurrence doesn't come along every day, and she gladly welcomed the opportunity to work with Bill. After several months of scheduling conflicts, we'd finally found a day that worked for everyone.

As we drew near the outskirts of Parkersburg, the car became quiet. The long-awaited moment was upon us.

Drifting Back in Time

"Okay, *now* I'm nervous," Bill sheepishly admitted as we pulled into the parking lot beside a wide, two-story Victorian-era house.

I'd seen these kinds of houses before. They are unmistakable. You can find them in nearly every city across the country—large, aging homes restored to their former glory and used as practice premises by doctors, dentists, and the like. I always thought it was a marvelous idea to make use of these older homes. It preserves the earlier charm and architecture of many neighborhoods and it's cheaper for doctors to renovate than to build. A "win-win" situation if there ever was one.

Opening the large front door and stepping inside, we were greeted very warmly by the receptionist. "Hello. Welcome to The Counseling House," she said. We introduced ourselves and within seconds other people appeared; and we were surrounded by a number of friendly faces, all female, enthusiastically extending their hands and smiling broadly. I'd rarely been treated to this much attention and I had the distinct feeling that Stephanie must have briefed the staff on our "little adventure". Bill and I felt like celebrities in the center of an admiring crowd.

Thirty-something, pert, and pretty, Stephanie was one of the first to step forward and introduce herself. Smartly dressed, she exuded both professional competence and the sweet demeanor of a kindergarten teacher, immediately putting us at ease.

After a few more pleasantries, we were ushered up an old winding staircase and into a small room on the front corner of the house. Sparsely furnished, it had a warm but clinical look about it. A large day-bed, adorned with a number of bright red pillows, dominated one side of the room. Opposite the day-bed were two cushioned chairs with a small table and lamp situated between them.

Stephanie invited Bill to sit on the day-bed, while she and I settled into the chairs. The air in the room nearly crackled with anticipation. Knowing we had only a limited amount of time, she got right down to business.

"Now I know you're probably a little excited, Bill, maybe a little nervous, but I want you to know that there's nothing to be afraid of here, okay?"

Fidgeting uncomfortably, an unconvincing, "Okay" was all Bill could manage.

"Do you have any questions you'd like to ask before we get started?"

"Only a few thousand," Bill replied, laughing and trying his best to look relaxed.

"Like I told you on the phone," she continued, "there's really nothing to be worried about. I'm just going to help you get into a trance state. This is simply a state of focused concentration in which you're deeply relaxed and more open to suggestion. This will allow us to explore the information stored in your subconscious mind and, hopefully, bring it out to the rational, conscious mind. That's really all we're doing. Do you understand?"

"I guess so. It just seems a little 'spooky', that's all."

"Spooky? I've had people use that word before. But honestly, most people don't realize they move in and out of hypnotic states and trances all the time in their everyday lives."

"They do?"

"Oh yes…all the time."

Sensing an opportunity to put Bill further at ease, Stephanie continued, "For example, when you drive your car down a highway, you zone out. You know you're on the road and you're aware of your surroundings—this feeling is comparable to the hypnotic trance. When you get lost in a good book or watching a movie, it's the same thing. So, today, we're not doing anything that you don't normally do almost every day. We're just doing it on purpose and we're going a little deeper. We'll use hypnosis to get you into a relaxed, trance-like state and then use a technique called 'age regression' to go back in your memory to a specific time. In this case, back to the accident when you were just five. That's all there is to it. Understand now?"

"I guess I understand it as well as I can…at the moment. It always looks like fun on TV," Bill said, laughing again with all the false gusto of a man about to climb into a dentist's chair.

"I'm not going to be clucking like a chicken when it's over, am I?"

"Not unless you clucked like a chicken before," she replied.

We all had a good laugh. Then our "little adventure" began in earnest.

"Now, Bill, I want you to lie back and get as comfortable on the bed as you can, okay?"

Giving me one final look as if to say, *I hope you know what I'm doing*, Bill grabbed one of the red pillows, put it under his head, and closed his eyes.

As the room grew quiet, I placed a small cassette tape recorder in the bed beside Bill and pushed the *Record* button, intending to capture for posterity whatever was going to happen, if anything. Opening the view finder on a video camera I borrowed from my son Matt, I settled back down in my chair and focused it on my brother, now lying comfortably on his back. I wasn't about to take any chances on a tape recorder malfunction and brought the video camera as a backup. One way or the other, I wanted a record of our session.

After a short prayer asking for God's protection and guidance, Stephanie reached over to the table and pressed a button on a small CD player, filling the room with soft, instrumental music. Then, over the next five minutes, using a technique called "guided imagery", she brought Bill step-by-step into a deep, relaxed, hypnotic state. It was fascinating to watch. To an amateur like me, it looked for all the world like Bill was sound asleep.

"Now, Bill, I would like you to go back in your mind to the day you were involved in a bad accident…at age five… go all the way back. Allow yourself to fall back in time before the first conversation you had with God…or Jesus. Are you there?"

There was no response. Bill seemed to be fast asleep, oblivious to his surroundings. Stephanie, an experienced therapist, knew not to force the question but waited patiently, letting Bill settle fully into the trance. After several minutes had passed, she asked again, "Bill, are you there?"

"Yes" came the reply.

"Okay. What do you see? Can you see anything?"

"There's a car…"

2

Flashback

February 26, 1970

I COULD FEEL THE cold…again…and I knew why. Without looking, I could sense his presence. Rolling slowly over onto my left side and lifting my eyelids ever so slightly, I could see him in the dim light of my room. There he was…again.

For the umpteenth time this winter and the second time this week, he had left his bed sometime in the wee hours and made his way to mine. He had evidently perfected the art of slipping silently under the covers, for he never once awakened me during his nighttime visitations. But I didn't mind. In fact, I rather liked finding my five-year-old brother huddled next to me on cold winter mornings. It made me feel…well, big brotherly.

Breathing slowly and rhythmically, I found him in his usual position that morning—on his left side, knees pulled tightly to his chest, with only the top of his head visible. He had perfected another art as well, one that was decidedly more annoying. Bundled to his eyeballs with the one blanket on my bed, Billy was peacefully ensconced under a small mountain of thick brown folds, leaving me with only a thin, white sheet to keep warm on this cold February morning. How he always managed to confiscate the entire blanket without rousing me, I'll never know. But this morning, like so many other mornings, I awoke half-chilled to find my little brother dozing securely beside me, enjoying the warmth and refuge of *my* blanket...again.

No matter. *Nothing is going to spoil this day*, I thought, as faint, gray light filtered through drawn curtains in the second-story bedroom I shared with my brother John. I grabbed a handful of blanket and, pulling it over my shoulder, rolled onto my right side, drifting back into a sweet, cozy slumber.

Sleep comes easily to twelve-year-old boys and I was planning on taking full advantage of that fact, especially today. Though it was a Thursday, no thoughts of school were there to disturb my morning, as the Kentucky Teachers Association (KTA) began its fourth day of a statewide strike, making every day this past week feel like a Saturday.

Though I will freely admit I was somewhat ignorant of the grand issues involved, I was nonetheless an unwavering supporter of the KTA's decision to declare a work stoppage. So staunch was my support that I was prepared, like many of my schoolmates, to stay out of school for the rest of the year if their demands—whatever they were—were not met. Yes, political involvement never felt so good.

The promise of fair skies that day by the local weatherman completed the dozy sense of anticipation I felt as I lay there. Warm winter days in northeastern Kentucky were an unusual treat for me and my neighborhood friends. It meant a day spent outside playing football in vacant lots, and generally staying on the verge of mischief until Mom's distant twilight call—Supper!—would pull me irresistibly homeward.

Even in my drowsy, half-conscious state, I could tell from the ever-brightening glow on the walls in my room that the sun was already cooperating with the weatherman's prediction. Yes, today was going to be a *very* good day.

Nothing in the Wind

Though sleeping-in was one of my favorite hobbies, the anticipated fun of the day ahead soon drew me out of bed and I found myself meandering slowly down the stairs, the last to join my siblings in our crowded kitchen. I was one of six children in the Anderson family, the second child and first son of Jim and Dorothy Anderson, a hard-working middle-class couple whose primary distinction in our middle-class neighborhood was having the largest brood on the block.

Unlike many who grow up on the edge of poverty, my recollections of childhood are always warm and pleasant, filled with good memories of life in a crowded but happy home where eight people shared one bathroom. Providing for six children was no doubt a tremendous strain on a one-income household, but if things ever got tight, I was blissfully unaware of it. I was loved and happy and that's all that really mattered.

The Anderson Siblings (1968). Clockwise from top: Diana, Jimmy, Johnny, Billy, Bobby, and Kathy

Rubbing the sleep from my eyes that morning, I watched carefully as my three brothers and two sisters busily buttered toast or poured milk on Cheerios. Being the last to arrive for breakfast in the Anderson house could be somewhat risky. In a large family, one learns to be quick about food or do with less, and occasionally, without. But I was in no hurry that morning. I had planned ahead.

Once everyone was seated at the table with their breakfast choices, I casually approached the large cabinet that housed our pots and pans. Trying to be as inconspicuous as possible, I reached inside and nonchalantly removed the packet of frosted Strawberry PopTarts I'd hidden in there the day before.

Experience had taught me that with a little ingenuity, one could enjoy a slightly more comfortable existence than one's siblings. An occasional excursion into petty larceny didn't hurt either.

Trying my best to tear open the packet as quietly as possible, I'd almost succeeded when my younger sister Kathy looked up from her cereal.

"Hey! Where'd you get those?" she protested, apparently not happy with my good fortune at finding such a tasty breakfast. "I thought they were all gone."

"Me too," I agreed, innocently, "but I opened the cabinet and there they were. I'm surprised no one else saw them."

Half-truths were a specialty of mine at that age.

But my sister knew me well.

"Which cabinet?" she asked.

"The cabinet over there," I said, nodding my head in the general direction of the cabinets.

"Which cabinet, Jimmy?" she countered, smelling a rat.

15

I decided to try a diversionary tactic.

"Look, I was the very last one down here, and if no one else saw these before I did, I can't see what all the fuss is about," I said, mounting a feeble defense.

She wasn't buying it.

"Which cabinet, Jimmy?"

I suddenly felt five pairs of eyes looking up at me from the table and I knew the jig was up. I decided to come clean.

"You know…" I said, pausing and smiling, "the one with the pots and pans."

"Mom!" came the instant response.

I grabbed my ill-gotten booty and quickly left the kitchen, laughing, before Mom could arrive to render justice.

No matter. I knew it was a tempest in a teapot and no harm would come. I also knew Pop-Tarts tasted just as good in my room as anywhere else. Maybe better.

Yeah, I thought to myself as I headed back upstairs, *it was going to be a very good day…*

Indeed, there was nothing in the wind to hint that this day wouldn't be just like any other day in my young life. There was nothing unusual in the morning routine, no ominous sense of foreboding, nothing out of place. Except for the sense of pure delight that being out of school brings to every child, the day felt as ordinary as a pair of white socks. Yet this clear and sunny February day stands out in my childhood memories like something from a horror movie—as lovely and beautiful a day as one could hope for

*in the middle of winter—suddenly, and without warning, turning
dark and bloody.*

Jimmy, age 8, and Billy, age 1 (1965)

An uneventful morning spent inside took a turn for the
better when my brothers and I headed outdoors after lunch.
I liked all my brothers and sisters, but Billy was always my
special little buddy; bright and cheerful, cute as a baby's butt,
and sharp as a tack. Being my youngest brother, I had taken
an unusual liking to Billy even as an infant, and the feelings
were reciprocated.

We spent countless hours playing together, and it

never bothered me in the least to have him tag along with me and my older neighborhood friends. I was his protector, his mentor, his playmate; I was his *big* brother, a role I deeply cherished. Everyone always said Billy seemed older than his five years. I suppose hanging around with his big brother, seven years his senior, had a way of rubbing off on him.

That particular afternoon, I had decided to shoot basketball at a goal across the alley behind our house. It was a net-less, makeshift affair that hung crooked from a neighbor's garage and was only nine feet off the ground. Billy, naturally, tagged along. He and I had played at this goal before. In fact, it was the only goal we'd ever played at because he wasn't yet strong enough to fling a basketball ten feet into the air. Nine feet was about the limit of his two-handed, between-the-legs heave. So it was a perfect setting for us to wile away a few minutes after lunch, waiting for neighborhood friends to appear.

Knowing full well that little Billy might not make a single basket, I decided to provide some motivation. "Tell you what I'll do," I said, as we walked out the back door, "I've got five pennies in my pocket and I'll give you one penny for every basket you make, okay?"

"You promise?"

"Promise?" I said, feeling slightly hurt that little Billy would question the honesty of his mentor. Then I remembered the Pop-Tart incident from earlier in the day and decided that perhaps my halo could stand a little straightening.

"Of course, I promise," I replied, with an earnest look and as much sincerity as I could stuff into four words. I meant it too.

"Okay, then!" he said with his trademark cheerfulness. "Let's go!"

With that, Billy took off through the back gate and darted up the alley.

The in-*cent*-ive (no pun intended) had just the effect I'd hoped for. When we parted twenty minutes later, I had three cents left in my pocket.

The Calm Before...

With the afternoon in full swing now, I made my way across the street in front of our house to a vacant lot that served double-duty as our sandlot football and baseball field. Football was the order of the day and soon my older neighborhood buddies and I were engrossed in one of the ten thousand games we played in that lot as youngsters. Not big enough to play with us, Billy decided to ride his Big Wheel, a gift from St. Nick, in the driveway that ran alongside our house.

As a young boy, that Big Wheel was one of his prized possessions. A sort of tricycle on steroids, it was a colorful, souped-up, low-slung, plastic monstrosity with an oversized wheel in the front. It was also equipped with a little device on the rear wheels that emitted a loud, and most annoying, *whrrrrrrrring* sound whenever the wheels turned. Santa had done well that past Christmas, or so we thought.

As the touchdowns piled up in the Super Bowl across the street, Billy was busying himself with his own Indy 500. Flying down the length of our driveway, pulling out into the street to turn around, and then hurtling back toward the garage as fast as his little five-year-old legs could peddle. He had schooled himself well in the art of putting on "the brakes"—jerking the front wheel to the side at full speed, and slinging the back end around in a perfect 180. Up and down, back and forth, he went in an endless oblong circuit, while passes were being thrown, caught, dropped, and intercepted on the other side of the street.

Monroe Street is a quiet, two-lane, residential thoroughfare running parallel to 29th Street, a much busier artery that cuts through the heart of South Ashland. About seven blocks long, Monroe was not distinctive in any way, except that it afforded a short-cut around an inconveniently-placed traffic light on 29th. More importantly to some, Monroe Street had no stop signs anywhere along its length. As such, it was a favorite of teenagers, those running late, and those with a need for speed. In the mornings before school and in mid-afternoon, it could resemble a drag-strip.

But on that afternoon, at that moment, all seemed well. My mother had just settled down in a rocking chair in her bedroom to catch her breath and a few minutes of quiet time after another long afternoon of housework. Five-foot-two on her best days, Mom was a human dynamo. Conscientious and hard-working, with more to do for eight people than one could ever squeeze into a mere twenty-four hours, I never knew my mother to sit for more than a few minutes at a time. But it would soon be time to start supper and, besides, she'd earned it.

Halfway across town, my father and his brother Frank had just slipped on their running shoes at the local YMCA and were on their way to the jogging track. As usual, my assorted siblings were scattered hither and yon, some inside, some outside. It was 4:53 PM. Yes, all was well.

As Billy completed another circuit up and back in the driveway, an errant football crossed Monroe Street and ended up in front of the Rothwell's house, our next-door neighbors. As the primary defender against that ill-thrown pass and the one closest to it, I instinctively headed across the street to retrieve it, head-down, with my thoughts focused on the game at hand. At just that moment, Billy spun his Big Wheel in a perfect 180-degree U-turn on the other side of Monroe Street and was starting to pedal back toward the driveway; and Tom Carver Jr., a 19-year-old young man in a yellow Volkswagen sedan, was heading south on Monroe in a hurry to get somewhere. The table was set.

...The Storm

The high-pitched screeching sound that rubber tires make when skidding across asphalt is quite unmistakable to the human ear, and at precisely seven minutes to five o'clock on Thursday, February 26, 1970, that unmistakable sound broke the neighborhood stillness with an unusually long and disquieting roar. Startled from light dozing, my mother heard it first and jumped to her feet. She knew her children were out there where that awful noise came from and instinctively flew to the front door.

On my way to retrieve our football, I was halfway across the street when I heard it—a loud, piercing scream in my left ear that broke my relaxed concentration and reflexively jerked my head toward the sound. What greeted my eyes when I turned my head was something straight from a nightmare—my little brother Billy pedaling serenely into the path of an oncoming yellow blur, then disappearing altogether at the sound of a heavy '*thud.*' As my mind struggled to comprehend what was happening, that yellow blur continued on in its path directly toward me, the whole scene bathed in the high-pitched roar of skidding tires.

What happened next remains somewhat of a mystery to me. In one instant, I was standing directly in the path of an oncoming yellow missile, frozen and immobile, and in the next instant, I was on the side of the street trying to recover my balance after feeling an impact on my lower left leg. I regained my feet quickly and, for a second or two, stood motionless trying to understand what had just happened.

Then I saw Billy, and everything in my young world was shattered. He lay motionless on his back on a bed of gravel in front of the Rothwell's house, about twenty feet from where I'd seen that yellow blur swallow him up. His prized Big Wheel, now an ugly piece of mangled plastic, lay just to his left.

I was the first to reach him, and the memory of what I saw in that brief moment haunts me to this day. He was lying on his back, his dark brown eyes staring up at me, fixed and unseeing, his arms slightly raised, his fingers curled around invisible handlebars. I'd never seen a dead person before, but I learned in that horrifying instant exactly what one looked like.

His head was oddly misshapen, his face ashen. He wasn't breathing. Blood trickled from his left ear. I remember the horrible sinking feeling that washed over me as I stood looking down at my little brother. Without thinking, I bent down to pick him up but drew back when frantic cries—Don't touch him!—reached my ears. Looking up, I saw several familiar faces running toward me as neighbors and friends came pouring out of their homes into the street, drawn by the shrieks and commotion.

Stepping backward, I stared in shock and horror at the unfolding scene. Woody Reed and Sandy Thornbury, neighbors from across the street, were the first to arrive. Sandy took one look at Billy and raced back to her house to call an ambulance. Woody, in a T-shirt and bare feet, kneeled down beside Billy and began massaging his chest in a desperate attempt to get him breathing again. Bessie Johnson, in her late seventies, approached within a few yards and turning hurriedly, rushed back to her house. Certain that little Billy was dead, she thought it best that the body be covered, and went to get a blanket.

The next few minutes were wholly unreal, a maelstrom of utter chaos, as scores of people appeared, children screamed and women cried, traffic became snarled, and in the distance, the plaintive wail of an ambulance siren growing, thankfully, ever louder.

Despite a growing sense of hopelessness, Woody continued to massage Billy's chest. After several minutes of concentrated effort, Billy suddenly gasped and began breathing again, much to the relief of those crowded around my brother as he lay there clinging to life on that cool February afternoon.

One enduring memory of those terrible moments is that of my poor mother, sobbing uncontrollably in the arms of Gene Salyers, a kindly neighbor from across the alley who was doing his dead-level-best to calm her and tell her that everything was going to be all right.

For a while, no one knew that I too had been hit by the car. I wasn't even really aware of it myself, as the raw energy and adrenaline that great trauma produces was coursing through my veins, numbing me to my own injury. At some point, I noticed that my left foot felt wet, as though I'd stepped in a puddle. Looking down, I was startled to see my left sneaker oozing blood. Only then did I realize that I

POLICE DEPARTMENT, ASHLAND, KENTUCKY
ACCIDENT REPORT

VEHICLE No. 1	VEHICLE No. 2
Time of Accident **4:53 P M** Date **2-26-70**	Place of Accident **2700 block Monroe**
Name of Driver **Thomas Parker Carver II**	Name of Driver **PEDESTRIANS: LISTED BELOW**
Address **3026 South 29th St Ashland, Ky**	Address **2732 Monroe**
Age **11-15-49** Sex **M** No. Driver L. **616792676876**	Age Sex No. Driver L.
No. Vehicle L. **94-338** State **Ky 69**	No. Vehicle L. State.
Kind of Vehicle **1968 VW**	Kind of Vehicle **PEDESTRIANS**
Owner **Thomas Parker Carver Sr**	Owner **n/a**
Defects of Vehicle **none**	Defects of Vehicle **n/a**
Incapacity of Driver **none**	Incapacity of Driver **n/a**
Violation of Traffic Regulations **none**	Violation of Traffic Regulations **none**
Street Conditions **dry blacktop**	Car Towed to: **none**
Weather Conditions **cool & sunny**	Released by: **none** Date

Probable Cause of Accident

Police Action: **none**   Arrest   Summons **none**   Assistance Rendered   **report made**

Persons Injured

	Name	Address	Age	Sex	Injury
1	Bill Anderson	2732 Monroe	5	M	taken to Cabell-Huntington
2	Jimmy Anderson	2732 Monroe	12	M	laceration of left leg
3					
4					
5					

Fault of Incapacity of Injured Person

Description of Accident and Damage

veh # 1 going south on 2700 block of Monroe - according to the driver, the two pedestrians came from his right side and quickly passed in front of his car causing the left front of his car to strike the two boys. Billy was on a tri-cycle and Jimmy was on foot.

damage to veh # 1: broken front headlight on left side. tri-cycle damaged on left side

veh # 1 skid marks: 66 feet

Witnesses	
Name	Address
none	none

Other Property Damage **none**

Attending Physician **Riestra**   Hospital **KDH**   Did Officer Witness Accident? **no**

Data Secured by: **Paul E True Jr**   Investigation   Witness   (OVER)

Police Report of the Accident

had been hurt, and that blood was running down my leg and into my shoe from a large cut on my left shin. Even then, I hardly felt it, as my eyes and thoughts were riveted on the pitiful little form still lying motionless in the gravel.

Life in the Balance

The arrival of an ambulance brought some welcomed relief to the pandemonium. As the paramedics began attending to my brother, I finally fell to the ground and began to examine my leg. Others then began to notice that I too was hurt and crowded around me. As the ambulance bearing Billy and my mother sped off for the local hospital, Agatha Gearhart, a gentle, middle-aged lady from up the street, volunteered to drive me to the hospital, and within seconds I was carried to her car for the short five-minute drive downtown. Another neighbor, unknown but appreciated, telephoned the YMCA and relayed the dreadful news to my father, who hurriedly dressed and left for the hospital in a brown business suit and white sneakers.

King's Daughter's Hospital was a 125-bed facility that served Ashland and its surrounding counties with good, general medical care, but was, at that time, unequipped to handle an injury of this magnitude. Dr. Evaristo Riestra, a Cuban immigrant and the attending emergency room physician that afternoon, found a most-gruesome sight as he removed the bandages from Billy's battered head.

The front bumper of the VW Sedan had struck my brother on the left side of his head, completely shattering the skull, and driving pieces of it into the brain with such force that brain tissue had been extruded out through his left ear canal. Dr. Riestra, knowing that the expertise and equipment to deal with this injury was not at his command, made the decision not to attempt any sort of treatment, but to transport him immediately to Cabell-Huntington Hospital, a much larger facility, 22 miles away.

As phone calls and arrangements were being hurriedly made, Dr. Riestra did perform one fateful and life-saving procedure. Suspecting massive internal bleeding, he discovered that Billy was in imminent danger of aspirating blood into his lungs and quickly suctioned his throat. Without his quick thinking and this one procedure, Billy would never have survived the trip to Huntington.

As X-rays were being taken of my left leg, my father and his brother arrived at the hospital just in time for Dad to climb into the ambulance for the torturous 20-minute race up Interstate 64 to West Virginia. Mom stayed behind with me and, when the X-rays showed no bone break, got the first bit of good news since the awful ordeal began, easily the worst hour in her thirty-two years. Thirteen stitches and a course of antibiotics and I would be as good as new, but neither of us felt like smiling, gripped as we were by the fearful uncertainty of what lay ahead.

Uncle Frank drove us home from the hospital to find a houseful of concerned relatives and well-meaning neighbors. No one had yet heard anything from my father, and an uneasy vigil began around the one telephone in our house.

We had very fine neighbors on Monroe Street, and food in a dozen different varieties was arriving in waves at the front door. Word of the accident had already spread far and wide. Thoughtful friends who knew of the Andersons also knew that Mrs. Anderson, who worked from sun-up to sun-down, could never begin to keep up the normal routine and cope with the crisis at hand, and were doing their best to help. The outpouring of sympathy, and food, was overwhelming. We never ate so well.

As the minutes dragged by like days, my dear mother grew frantic to hear something...anything. The strain eventually became too great to bear and at 9:00 PM, my grandfather, Art Anderson, my Uncle David, and Mom set out for the hospital in Huntington. Forty-five long minutes later, they found the surgical waiting area, darkened and deserted, except for my father, sitting pensively in the corner of the room with a worried look on his face. A large and imposing man, Dad rarely let his emotions show, but the stress of the last few hours was clearly evident on his face.

After a long-needed embrace, my mother asked, "Where's Billy?"

"Still in surgery," came the solemn reply. "The nurse was just here and told me he should be out soon...nothing other than that."

Holding hands, they sat down together and tried to catch their breath, finally able to lean on each other and relax a little after hours of facing the trauma separately. In the midst of the turmoil, it was comforting to be together again. Hungry for more information, they hurriedly exchanged their stories of the preceding five hours, Mom telling Dad what she remembered of the accident and Dad relating events in the ambulance and at the hospital.

Buoyed by each other's presence and somehow feeling slightly more optimistic, they were still trying to fit all the pieces together when a figure appeared in the doorway of the room...

3

Anywhere Else on Earth

Dr. Thomas J. Holbrook, of Holbrook, Lobo, & Sakhai, was just getting ready to leave his downtown office a little before six o'clock that day when his secretary informed him that an urgent call had just come from Cabell-Huntington Hospital. A severe head injury case from Ashland would arrive at the hospital within minutes, and he was asked to attend.

Quickly canceling plans for the evening, he headed to the hospital to await his new patient, hoping as always that the full range of his skills as a neurosurgeon would not be needed. Five grueling hours later, he stood a few feet from two weary parents, preparing to give them a report on his handiwork and an assessment of their youngest son's chances of survival.

Death at the Door

Frozen in mid-sentence, Dad instinctively rose to his feet as Dr. Holbrook quietly entered the waiting room, still wearing an operating gown. Mom quickly followed, grasping Dad's left arm for the support she knew she would need.

The air was suddenly charged with tension. The awful moment of truth—the reality of life or death—had arrived. Both took a halting step forward, feeling their pulses quicken, and trying to brace themselves for whatever the next few minutes would bring. Papaw and Uncle David, sitting quietly together a few feet away, rose as well but kept a respectful distance.

Dispensing with any formalities, he got right to the point. "Mr. and Mrs. Anderson, I'm Dr. Holbrook," he began. "You have a very seriously injured child. The impact to his head produced a compound, depressed fracture of the skull and a major laceration of the brain. There was a lot of splintered bone and all I could basically do was to clean up the wound, relieve the cranial pressure, remove damaged tissue, and reconstruct the skull as best I could. He has lost a lot of brain tissue. There is also some damage to his left ear and left eye. However, on the plus side, he has no other broken bones."

Glancing down at the clipboard in his left hand, he continued, "The major thing I'm concerned about at the moment is the post-operative swelling of his head. We will be monitoring that very closely. Right now, he is in a deep coma, but that is best for the time being. We'll just have to wait and see what happens in the next twenty-four hours."

Practiced at giving hard news and knowing not to overwhelm two already-distraught parents, he paused momentarily to let all the information sink in. Then, with as much compassion as he could put in his voice, he delivered the stunner, "We lost him three times in pre-op and were able to bring him back each time."

At that, Dad felt the grip on his left arm suddenly tighten as Mom's knees turned to water. Struggling to keep her composure and drawing a sharp gasp of air, she staggered. The news was almost too much to bear after the trauma of the last few hours.

Speaking in quiet, deliberate tones, Dr. Holbrook continued, "I'm really very sorry, but I can give you no guarantees. We did all we could do, but I don't really expect him to live through the night."

For Jim and Dorothy Anderson, time suddenly seemed to stand still. Staring straight ahead, with eyes glazed and unseeing, a feeling of numbness quietly swept over them as the awful news hit home. From deep within, faint voices whispered, *Can this really be happening? Surely this is just a nightmare that I'll soon awake from.* But the numbness quickly faded and brutal reality flooded back at full force.

Dad recovered first. "When can we see him?" he asked.

"He's in post-op right now. I'll have a nurse take you to the ICU in just a few minutes." As he turned to leave, Dr. Holbrook reached out and placed a supportive hand on Mom's shoulder. Instinctively wishing he could soften the impact of his prognosis, he said, "I'm really very sorry. I hate to see little children injured."

Through tear-filled eyes came the heart-felt response, "Thank you, Doctor…for all you've done."

Knowing there was no more to say, Dr. Holbrook slipped quietly away, leaving two shaken parents to come to grips with the realization that death was yet standing at the Family door and that life would never be quite the same again.

Jim and Dorothy Anderson (1979)

Anywhere Else on Earth

Within minutes, a young female figure appeared at the same door where Dr. Holbrook had disappeared, and said softly, "Mr. and Mrs. Anderson, if you'll come with me, I'll take you to the ICU where you can see your son."

Leaving Papaw and Uncle David in the stillness of the darkened waiting room, they made their way through a maze of well-lit corridors and into the glare of the Intensive Care Unit. Ushered into a large, warm room filled with medical equipment and monitors, and partitioned into smaller areas by hanging drapes, the nurse asked them to wait inside the door and someone in the ICU would take them to see Billy.

In a matter of seconds, another nurse appeared, introduced herself, and told them that she was sorry but they could only stay for just a few minutes. With that, she turned and walked a few steps to one of the partitioned areas and drew back the curtain slightly, saying politely, "He's in here."

Dad felt Mom's fingers reach for his hand and close around it in a viselike grip. Pausing momentarily to steady themselves and drawing a deep breath, they walked together those grim few paces to the edge of the curtain. Wishing they could be anywhere else on Earth, they hesitantly stepped inside.

Hearing the nurse slowly draw the curtain closed, their eyes fell upon the small pitiful form lying on his back

CABELL HUNTINGTON HOSPITAL
HISTORY AND PHYSICAL EXAMINATION

Anderson, William D.   181038

T. J. Holbrook, M. D.   2-26-70   232F

This 5-year old boy, according to the father had had no serious illness, or upheaval in health. No history of allergies, hay fever, or known drug sensitivities. When perhaps about 4:30 or 4:45 p.m. this afternoon, he had apparently been struck by a car while playing. The details are not known, but at any rate, he had evidently been unconscious since that time and had been transferred here from King's Daughters Hospital.

On neurological examination, he is in an unconscious state, but does turn from side to side. When the bandages are removed, there are multiple lacerated wounds in the left parieto-occipital area, the longest of which is about an inch in size and there is active bleeding from the left ear. Likewise, a specimen from the ER. is available of obvious brain tissue which amounts to an estimated cubic cm. of gray matter and white matter. The left ear was cleansed and in the external ear, there was a small fragment of tissue which had the appearance of brain tissue, but whether it came from the ear or other location and got in the ear is uncertain. The pupils respond slowly. The right is slightly smaller than the left, but they are not very much different in size. There is much swelling about the left eye with hematomatous change without abrasion. On stimulation, he is with obvious moderate right facial weakness and some weakness of the right arm. He has no response to plantar stimulation. Pulse 68, BP. 106/60. The heart appears to be of normal size, rhythm regular. No abnormality of the lung fields made out. The abdomen appears soft. There is an abraded area in the right costal margin at about the midaxillary line region.

IMPRESSION:
Laceration of the brain. X-rays have shown fracture of the skull - compound fracture of the skull, left parietal, probable basal skull fracture with aural hematorrhea. Multiple lacerated wounds, left fronto-occipital.

The patient's state is a critical circumstance from brain injury. He is admitted to ICU. for further management.

T. J. Holbrook, M. D/gw/2-March-70.

CHH Patient Examination Report

in a large, white bed inside a glass-fronted isolation unit. Nearly naked, with tubes and IVs running everywhere and surrounded by a battery of life support equipment, little Billy was almost unrecognizable. His bandaged head was nearly double its normal size and his blackened eyes were swollen shut. With only the rhythmic sound of the respirator in the background, Jim and Dorothy Anderson stood silently, almost reverently, looking down at their youngest son, while the full gravity of the moment flooded in upon them with irresistible force.

Feeling helpless and overwhelmed, the sight became more than Mom could bear. Turning suddenly, she buried her face into Dad's shoulder, releasing all the pent-up emotions of a mother's heart. "Oh, Dear God...Dear God..." she pleaded as tears of quiet desperation flowed freely down her cheeks.

Fighting back his own tears and knowing that she needed him to be strong, Dad put his arms around his hurting wife and drew her close. Feeling the same helplessness, he knew there was really nothing he could say to ease the crushing pain. For a moment or two, they stood transfixed, eyes closed, leaning on each other for strength, and wondering how on Earth they could ever endure the night.

Hearing the nurse approach, they separated, looking back again at their youngest son, clinging to life just a few feet away. Knowing that time was nearly gone, their minds began to race...*how small and fragile he looks in that immense bed...is he feeling any pain?...how cruel and unfair it is for a child to suffer like this...will this be the last time I see my son alive?* As these and other thoughts came flashing through their minds, the sharp noise of steel rings sliding on steel rods could be heard as the nurse slowly pulled the curtain back open.

"Mr. and Mrs. Anderson, could we please get some information from you before you leave?" she asked, subtly informing them that visiting time was over.

Taking one long, last look at Billy, they followed her back to the front desk, answered a few cursory questions on Billy's medical history, and gave her our home phone number. After dutifully recording the answers, she said in soft, sympathetic tones, "We'll call you right away if there is any change. I'm very sorry."

Two Pennies for Luck

Leaving the ICU, they were making their way slowly and deliberately back through the maze of corridors when they heard a female voice shouting from behind, "Mr. and Mrs. Anderson!" Turning to see the ICU nurse in hot pursuit, they felt their pulses quicken, hoping against hope that she was not bearing bad news.

"I'm *so* sorry," she began, "I completely forgot to give you this." Breathing a welcomed sigh of relief, it was then that they saw she carried a small bag. "These are your son's clothes" she said, placing the bag in Mom's hand. Pausing for a brief instant, she continued, "And…we also found these in one of his pockets." Extending a hand, palm up, she produced two round, copper pennies, Billy's basketball winnings from earlier that day.

Dropping the pennies into Mom's hand, she quickly

turned and, running back nearly as fast as she came, said, "I've *got* to get back."

"Thank you...thank you..." came Mom's automatic reply as the nurse disappeared around a corner. Then, glancing back down at the two dark copper coins in her palm, Mom had a revelation.

My mother was not a superstitious woman, yet somehow, in the desperation of the hour, she suddenly saw in those two pennies something different—a sign, an omen. *Somehow*, she thought, *this means 'good luck.'*

In life's darkest hours, the human mind will sometimes grasp at anything, however meaningless, as an anchor of hope. To Dorothy Anderson, these two coins, tucked away in Billy's pockets at the moment of impact, became the anchor she needed. She had no idea where he got them, all she knew was that these two pennies meant that somehow, some way, all would be well. It meant 'good luck.' It just had to.

Closing her hand around those pennies and squeezing them as if her life depended on it, Mom silently promised herself that she was going to hold on to those coins until little Billy was well again. Looking up at Dad with a vaguely hopeful look in her eyes, and somehow feeling a little better, she said, "I'm so tired...let's go home."

4

Facing the Dawn

OUR HOUSE AT 2732 Monroe Street, where eight people lived in nine rooms, was usually a place of peaceful chaos. The evening of February 26, 1970, was no different, only more so. With Mom and Dad at the hospital in Huntington, an assortment of relatives—aunts, uncles, and cousins—descended upon us in a steady torrent. Reports of the accident had spread quickly through the Family grapevine and the small house where we lived was literally bursting with people.

My grandmother, Margaret Anderson, and Uncle David's wife, Pat, had taken charge of me and my siblings, and were also dealing with the endless parade of well-meaning visitors. Food continued to arrive at the front door and pile up at an alarming rate in our little kitchen.

Worst of all, a non-stop tangle of concerned calls kept our one phone line constantly busy. Having heard nothing from Dad or Mom all evening, everyone's nerves were on edge and every ring of the phone, which seemed to happen at regular three minute intervals, sent everyone into a frenzy.

Aunt Pat quickly became adept at handling the incoming calls. Whenever a call turned out to be from some concerned neighbor or friend, she would thank them for calling, give a quick thirty-second update, and then politely but firmly say we needed to keep the line open. With so much practice, she eventually got the routine down to ten seconds, and finally, could do it all in one sentence.

Long Dark Night

My own recollections of that evening, aside from the general turmoil, are a bit fuzzy. I seem to recall my leg beginning to throb as the evening wore on, and taking great care not to bump it or walk on it heavily. I'd never had stitches before, so it was a new experience for me. It was also the first time in my young life that I can recall feeling anxious. If I'd ever felt a bit nervous before, it was only for very brief moments. It was nothing like the intense cloak of anxiety that blanketed me that night.

In one sense, I am thankful that the evening is a blur in my memory, but I do have one rather vivid recollection. I recall my grandmother trying her best to shuttle us all off to bed somewhere in the vicinity of ten o'clock. But dealing with five youngsters is not an easy thing to do when one has been out of practice. However, my grandmother was nothing if not persistent, and eventually we were all safely in bed by ten-thirty.

Tired but not sleepy, I remember reluctantly climbing the steps and crawling into my cold little wagon-wheel bed. But going to bed and going to sleep are two different things when haunted by the distresses of the day, and sleep was thoroughly elusive. Without any effort on my part, the terrible scenes of that day played in a long endless loop in the theater of my mind. Without a moment of peace, I laid restlessly in the inky blackness of my bedroom for what seemed like a short eternity.

Then suddenly, about midnight, I heard the sound of a car pulling into our driveway. Bum leg or not, I raced downstairs at the speed of light, and was waiting at the back door even before my grandmother and Aunt Pat could walk the twelve steps from our den to the kitchen. As the back door to our house swung open, I blurted out the one agonizing question that had filled my mind for hours. "Is he still alive?" I asked intently.

"Yes," was my dad's one-word reply.

Hearing his answer but hungering for more, I asked again, "He's still alive?"

At that, my mom, who sensed the overwhelming distress in her oldest son, walked over and put her arms around me. "Yes, Jimmy, he's still alive," she said in calm, motherly tones. "He was in surgery for four hours but he made it through, and now we just have to wait."

Seeing my reaction and feeling she must not mislead me, she added the cryptic words, "But, yes…at the moment…

he's still alive."

However well-intentioned my mom's subtle message was, it never registered on me. I was on cloud nine. I remember the moment vividly because I felt the weight of the entire world fall off my young shoulders. In the simple logic of my twelve-year-old mind, that settled the issue—he was going to live and that was all that mattered. I was ecstatic. *Surely, I reasoned, if Billy could live for seven hours after being hit in the head by a car, he's got to be over the worst of it...he'll live now...no doubt about it.*

Innocently oblivious to the reality of the situation but feeling immensely happier, I stood in the kitchen for a few more minutes while "the grown-ups" talked. But I never really heard anything they were saying. I had all the answers I needed. Ushered off to bed moments later, I remember laying there for a few minutes rejoicing on the inside, before drifting off into a peaceful slumber.

Downstairs, it was a different matter. After giving a brief update to all present, followed by a hasty but sincere "thank-you and good-night," Dad and Mom collapsed in the den. Too exhausted to eat or think, they settled in quiet heaps on the couch. Thankful to be back home, but too overwrought to enjoy it, my parents spent the entire night in restless conversation, waiting for the phone to ring.

Either way the drama played out, there was much to discuss and much to plan. Knowing it was useless to get in bed, they dozed lightly when there was a lull in the conversation. While I slept peacefully upstairs, Mom and Dad spent a torturous night wrestling with matters of life and death, huddled together near the phone, hoping to God it wouldn't ring.

Thankfully, it never did.

Facing the Dawn

When the first rays of the sun peeked over the frosty hills of eastern Kentucky the following morning, Jim and Dorothy Anderson were already halfway between Ashland and Huntington. Physically and emotionally drained, yet buoyed by the knowledge that Billy had survived the night, they headed back to Cabell Huntington Hospital with equal measures of apprehension and hope. At the same time, Aunt Pat was sitting down with a cigarette and a cup of coffee amidst the smorgasbord in our kitchen, ready to resume her watch over the Anderson brood as the Kentucky Teachers' strike entered its fifth day.

Turning off of 16th Street and into the hospital parking lot, everything seemed different. The hospital's edifice, so dark and ominous the previous night, looked noticeably less imposing in the gray light of a crisp winter morning, as Dad and Mom quickly made their way from the parking lot to the ICU. Hopeful that Billy's condition had improved, they felt their pulses begin to race slightly as they opened the heavy, double-doors that fronted the Intensive Care Unit.

"He had a peaceful night," the Charge Nurse told them, looking down at Billy's chart. "His vital signs are relatively stable and it appears that the post-op swelling, which is our biggest concern, has not gotten any worse over the last few hours. But he's still in very critical condition. Dr. Holbrook should be here shortly. If you'd care to step back out into the waiting area, I'll let him know you are here when he arrives."

"Can we see Billy?" asked Dad.

"Yes, but not at the moment," she answered. "They're changing his dressing. Visitation in the ICU can only be for ten minutes at a time every two hours," she added. "You can see him at nine."

Counting the minutes, Dad and Mom stood again at the nurse's desk at precisely nine o'clock and were quickly ushered to Billy's bedside. Better prepared than the previous night, they kept their emotions in check and stood quietly, gazing with loving tenderness on their youngest son, still in the grasp of a deep coma, on the very edge of life. No words were spoken. None were really needed. Mom, clutching those two precious pennies in her hand, looked hopefully up at Dad as they were leaving and whispered in wishful tones, "I think his color is better."

Dr. Holbrook, pleasant and sympathetic as always, added little to the Charge Nurse's report when he arrived at nine-thirty. "We're doing all we can," he said. "The fact that he's stable right now is a good sign. But there's nothing to be done except to wait and see what happens over the next twenty-four hours."

Guardedly optimistic to hear that little Billy was holding his own, and grateful for any small victory, Dad and Mom resigned themselves to a long, tiring day of shuttling from the ICU waiting room to Billy's bed, and back again. Catnapping between visits, they took full advantage of the day to rest as much as possible and refine their plans for the next few days. With five children at home, Mom and Dad knew that they couldn't both spend every day at the hospital.

Sweet Innocence

Back in Ashland, the Anderson household had calmed down somewhat from the circus of the previous night. Food continued to amass and phone calls came in regularly, but at a much slower pace. I recall the mood in the house being rather somber, with my brothers and sisters and myself quietly playing inside all day. Of course we all knew that Billy had been terribly injured and might die, but as youngsters mostly under the age of ten, we didn't really comprehend the gravity of the situation.

With all the furor of the last twenty-four hours, there had really been no time for anyone to sit down with us and explain the full extent of what was happening. We simply gathered what we could from overhearing conversations and phone calls. Whether by circumstance or by design, it was probably best that we didn't know. Looking back, I'm sure Dad and Mom didn't want to further complicate matters by creating a houseful of overly-stressed children, and kept as much of the bad news from us as possible.

In the sweet innocence and optimism of youth, we all seemed to carry the unspoken assumption that since Billy hadn't died after the accident, he'd recover and be home in a few days. At least, that's what my heart wanted to believe, and I did my best to convince my siblings, and myself, of the same. Little did we know that he was far from being 'out of the woods.'

Celebrity

I was not accustomed to having people know my name. Like most twelve-year-olds, I was thoroughly anonymous. Except for Little League baseball exploits and a poster contest, my name had never appeared with any prominence in the local newspaper. But when the evening edition of *The Ashland Daily Independent* arrived that day, I found, to my utter surprise, that I had achieved celebrity status.

There, plastered on the front page no less, was an article on yesterday's accident. There, in black and white, for thousands to read, was my name, along with Billy's of course. I remember reading the story over and over and over. I couldn't take my eyes off of it. Despite the fact that the article described all the horrid events of the previous day, there was my name—Jimmy Anderson—right on the front page of the paper for everyone to see and enjoy. And enjoy it I did.

Then, right on the heels of the newspaper, came the six o'clock evening news on WSAZ Channel 3 and, there again, to my great astonishment was a story on the accident. Without warning, there was my name again, broadcast in living color to every household in the tri-state. How I exulted. *Wow*, I thought, *everyone will know who I am now*, as a wholly unexpected feeling of importance coursed through my being.

Of course, I wasn't really happy about the tragic way it happened, but I must admit that the fleeting sense of fame I enjoyed at that moment was a refreshing mental diversion and did wonders to relieve the tension I was feeling. Unfortunately, it didn't last too long. When Dad and Mom arrived back home after dark that evening, without better news, I found myself toiling under the same feeling of apprehension and struggling to tell myself, yet again, that Billy would soon be back home, safe and sound.

From Every Hill and Hollow

Apart from providing my twelve-year-old psyche a much-needed boost, the wide publicity that our accident received had a much more profound and lasting effect. What followed in the wake of the newspaper and television reports was an outpouring of support and sympathy, particularly from area churches, that was instant and overwhelming.

Beginning slowly that evening and building for days afterward, we were literally engulfed in a wave of love and attention. From every hill and hollow in the tri-state, came a flood of cards, letters, phone calls, and impromptu visits from concerned and well-meaning people. Offers of help covered the full range of human activity, from doing our laundry to feeding our cats, and everything else in between. On top of the help we were already getting from family and friends, this outpouring of support did much to buoy our spirits and provided a much-needed sense that we were not facing the struggle alone.

Living in the heart of the Bible Belt, a steady stream of pastors, elders, deacons, bishops, priests, and laity, from every denomination and creed, began arriving at our front door to offer their sympathy and support and, most importantly, their prayers. I can remember standing in our den while men I did not know laid their hands on me and prayed.

Each day our mail chute was stuffed with letters and cards from various churches, Sunday school classes and Bible study groups, all expressing their concern and letting us know that they would be praying for those two young Anderson boys. We even received cards from churches in other states, the furthest one coming, unbelievably, from a church in Massachusetts. It was astounding.

I think it would be fair to say that, in 1970, the Andersons were not the most "religious" family in town, or indeed, even on our block of Monroe Street. We weren't non-believers, but we were nominal Christians at best. We did attend the local Episcopal Church on a sporadic basis, but we were Biblically-illiterate and devoid of prayer.

As such, we were spiritually ill-prepared for the life-and-death battle we found ourselves in. Thankfully for us, however, as word of the accident spread, area churches and countless individual Christians began supplying the one vital ingredient that was sorely lacking in the struggle—intercessory prayer.

It wouldn't be until years later that I learned of the indispensable value and power of intercessory prayer when faced with Satan's onslaught. In my own mind, there is no doubt that the prayer of faith (James 5:15-16), offered by hundreds, maybe thousands, was the unseen force that eventually turned the battle in our favor and opened the door for God's power to be manifested in an indisputable and miraculous way.

Both Sides of the Street

Over the next several days, things settled into a holding pattern of sorts. With Billy still in a coma, stable but critical, Dad and Mom thought it best if someone from the family could stay with him around the clock. When my Aunt Pat, ever eager to help when problems arose, volunteered to stay at the hospital during the day, Dad began twice daily trips to Huntington.

In the mornings he would drive up with Pat and come

back with Mom and do the reverse in the evenings. Mom catnapped at the hospital during the night and did her best to keep up the house and attend to us kids during the day. It was an unbelievable grind, but the housework tended to be somewhat therapeutic, as it helped to keep her mind off the unfolding drama.

On my part, I felt rather lost. I tried my best to resume the normal playful activities of a twelve-year-old boy, but my heart wasn't in it. I had thirteen stitches in my leg, but it was my head that was giving me trouble. I loved my little brother very much and the all-pervading concern I felt for him simply smothered me and robbed me of my usual carefree disposition. Both of my parents noticed it and, despite their preoccupation with events in Huntington, did their best to guide me through it, albeit with completely contradictory advice.

Dad, stalwart and ever the man-of-the-house, told me privately to be strong and to resist the temptation to cry and be overly-emotional. Mom, on the other hand, gave me polar-opposite advice, and quietly cautioned me not to hold my emotions inside but to let them flow freely, but discreetly.

Faced with parental contradiction of such monumental proportions, I did what any confused but self-respecting adolescent would naturally do—I was tough and strong when Dad was around and cried my eyes out when Mom was around. Oblivious to each other's council, both seemed pleased that I had embraced their advice.

Sometimes it's just easier to walk both sides of the street.

5

Miracle on 16th Street

WHEN BILLY REMAINED STABLE through the weekend, Dr. Holbrook discontinued life-support and downgraded his condition from critical to serious. On Monday, he had him moved from the ICU to a "step-down" unit. These "step-down" units, as the name implies, were small, private rooms designed for patients who no longer warranted ICU care but still had specialized nursing needs. Being private, these units had one tremendous advantage over the ICU—they allowed family members to stay with patients, giving Mom and Aunt Pat an opportunity to be in the same room with Billy twenty-four hours a day.

During this time, Dr. Holbrook and his colleagues were also conducting a detailed and comprehensive assessment of Billy's injuries. From both a medical and legal standpoint, it was necessary to determine what limitations and handicaps Billy would likely have should he survive the accident. If he ever regained consciousness, it was obvious that he would have a number of serious and permanent handicaps that would require lifelong attention.

Dr. Holbrook, thorough and professional as always, knew it was time to sit down with Dad and Mom to explain Billy's injuries in some detail and what likely outcomes they could expect. Knowing that a hospital waiting room was a poor setting for such a discussion, he asked them to meet with him at his downtown office on Tuesday afternoon.

Losing Hope

Arriving slightly ahead of their 2:00 PM appointment, Dad and Mom were warmly greeted by Dr. Holbrook's secretary and ushered into a large, spacious office. "Dr. Holbrook is running a little late," she explained. "He should be here anytime. Could I get you some coffee?"

Politely declining her offer, they settled into the soft leather chairs that sat in front of Dr. Holbrook's dark mahogany desk. Mom, still carrying the lucky pennies, found it too difficult to sit still and got up to pace the floor. Knowing that Billy had stabilized and was somewhat improved, they both carried secret hopes that Dr. Holbrook had better news to give them. It wasn't to be.

"So sorry to keep you waiting," Dr. Holbrook said as he burst into his office. "You never really know when you'll be able to leave the hospital."

Tall and courtly, with wire-rim glasses and graying temples, Dr. Holbrook looked every inch the image of an experienced neurosurgeon. His voice had a calming yet authoritative and knowledgeable quality that inspired confidence and compelled the listener to accept every word without question.

Thomas J. Holbrook, M.D.

Vanderbilt-educated, Thomas Holbrook came to Huntington in 1949 and established the city's first neurosurgical practice. Later, he served as Chief of Neurology and Neurosurgery at St. Mary's Hospital and created the hospital's first encephalography unit. Nationally-recognized as a medical scholar, Dr. Holbrook had numerous articles appear in the medical journals, *Surgery* and *Archives of Surgery*. He was also a founding member of the Neurosurgical Society of America and the American Board of Electroencephalography.

A devout Christian, Dr. Holbrook was universally admired for the breadth of his scientific and medical knowledge, his unrivaled skill in the delicate field of neurosurgery, and for his warm bedside manner, a combination of qualities all too rare in modern medicine.

So renowned was Dr. Holbrook as an expert in the field of neuroscience that he received an emergency call in November of 1963 and was asked to attend to President Kennedy after the assassination attempt by Lee Harvey Oswald. Sadly, the President died before he could board a hastily-chartered flight for Dallas.

Call it good luck or God's Providence, little Billy was certainly fortunate to have one of the world's most gifted and accomplished neurosurgeons in practice just 22 miles from his home in Ashland.

Thanking Dad and Mom for coming and expressing his sympathies for what had happened, Dr. Holbrook briefly explained his reasons for the meeting and then presented them with a neatly-typed, two-page report on his assessment of one William David Anderson, age 5.

Using anatomical models in his office, he reviewed the report line by line, showing them the nature and extent of Billy's injuries. It was a gruesome list:

1. *Injuries:*

a. *Compound, comminuted depressed fracture of the skull, left side;*

b. *Severe laceration of the left cerebral hemisphere of the brain;*

c. *Intracerebral hemorrhage, left side, with extrusion of cerebral tissue from the ear;*

d. *Incomplete right-sided paralysis;*

e. *Shock due to trauma;*

f. *Laceration of the scalp, left side, with associated abrasions and contusions.*

Worse still, Dr. Holbrook's assessment of what those injuries would entail, should Billy survive and regain consciousness, was frightening:

2. *Physical Damage:*

a. *Coma, partial paralysis, loss of memory — potentially permanent and irreversible;*

b. *Partial loss of right-side visual field — permanent and irreversible;*

c. *Partial loss of hearing, left side — permanent and irreversible;*

d. *Loss of brain tissue (does not regenerate) — permanent and irreversible;*

e. *Scarring from depressed fracture and surgery — permanent and irreversible.*

3. *Future Impairments:*

a. *Complications — strong possibility of epilepsy, tumors, and retardation;*

b. *Education limitations — difficulty with numbers, symbols, and concentration;*

c. *Employment limitations due to physical handicaps listed above;*

d. *Living limitations — operation of vehicles and machines, care of self, etc.;*

e. *Costs — periodic examinations, costs of future complications.*

Dad and Mom sat in stunned silence as Dr. Holbrook proceeded through the report. Nothing had prepared them for this. Cautiously optimistic that Billy would survive the accident, they suddenly came to see just what that might mean.

Overwhelmed by the avalanche of bad news, they both felt the last glimmer of hope fade away as Dr. Holbrook concluded his report by saying, "At this point, we can do nothing more for him. It's really all in the hands of The Man Upstairs. Your son might regain consciousness or he may stay in a permanent, vegetative state. No one can know. It's still just a wait-and-see situation."

Pausing slightly, he added the chilling words, "But frankly…I think it would be better if he did not survive."

Though the winter sun was shining brightly through the wide office windows that day, Jim and Dorothy Anderson felt a numbing darkness descend upon them, as a parent's worst nightmare was laid out before them in brutal detail. As before, time seemed to stop as faint thoughts began to echo randomly in their minds, *Surely to God this can't be happening... he's so young...it's not fair...how can God let this happen?* Jolted suddenly back to reality when Dr. Holbrook's phone rang, Dad and Mom knew there was no reason to stay any longer. Wanting to escape that office as quickly as possible, they thanked Dr. Holbrook for everything he'd done and quickly excused themselves.

Shattered by the news, Dad and Mom drove the 25 minutes back to Ashland in silence, each lost in their own thoughts. Sensing that the battle had become hopeless and tired of fighting, Mom broke the spell as Dad pulled into the driveway, saying rather philosophically, "Well, at least we'll have five kids left."

Foreshadow

Wednesday, March 4, 1970 dawned overcast and gloomy, in more ways than one. The Kentucky Teachers' strike had ended the day before, and Ashland Public Schools were back in session for the first time in nearly two weeks. Needless to say, I wasn't overjoyed.

I was a good student and I liked school generally, but with my leg still in stitches and my brother still in a coma, I knew I would be too distracted to concentrate on my studies.

Unbelievably, with Mom at the hospital, my four siblings and I all managed to get ourselves up and off to school on time—a genuine miracle in itself. It must have been a prelude of things to come. As it turned out, it was just the beginning of miracles that day.

Dad was following the usual routine. He left for Huntington with Aunt Pat about 7:30 and returned with Mom about 9:30. If he was lucky, he'd be there when Dr. Holbrook made his rounds. But more often than not, it was Mom who got the chance to talk to Dr. Holbrook, who liked to see his patients early in the morning before he got busy in surgery.

As for Billy, he remained in the "step-down" unit, fully stable but not showing any distinct signs of improvement. He was still in a deep coma and unresponsive to stimuli. His breathing was shallow and though fed through a stomach tube, he was losing weight. The tremendous swelling of his head, life-threatening and grotesque, had subsided greatly, and his eyes, still black, were only slightly swollen now. It had been six days since the accident and little Billy had not moved a muscle.

For my parents, each day was a struggle. To see their youngest child, once so energetic and full of life, now so small and pitifully frail, was heartrending. The constant sense of tension, coupled with the physical demands of being at the hospital day-in and day-out, was mentally and emotionally exhausting. But worst of all, they were forced to labor under the cruel knowledge that there was no way out, no escape from the drama, until it played itself out—one way or another.

Miracle on 16th Street

That particular March afternoon was unusually mild, with temperatures climbing into the mid-sixties—a welcomed respite from the cold. Dad spent the day in his office at Beneficial Finance, while my siblings and I, scattered randomly between the second and tenth grades, got re-acquainted with our schools. Mom, on the other hand, made good use of our absence at home to catch up on her rest.

Aunt Pat spent the day sitting next to Billy, reading magazines, watching TV, and listening to a small transistor radio she always took with her. She had become friendly with the nurses who frequented Billy's room and took advantage of their visits for short walks in the hallway to relieve the boredom and stretch her legs. This day was a carbon copy of the one before and the one before that. Nothing seemed particularly different. Like all the days before, Billy hadn't stirred or made a single sound. It was starting to look like he never would.

At 4:40, Pat returned to his room after a quick trip to the canteen for a late-afternoon Milky Way bar. In another hour or so, Dad and Mom would make their welcomed appearance. It had been another long day and Pat was eager to get home. Gazing out the third-floor window with WKEE playing in the background, she thought she heard a faint noise, like the rustle of bed sheets, but paid no heed. Spending five straight days in Billy's room, she had grown accustomed to the constant noise that is part of every hospital setting and, besides, she was tired.

Reaching down for a magazine beside her chair, she caught a glimpse of movement in the corner of her eye and, turning her head quickly, got the shock of her life—there was little Billy sitting straight up and looking her right in the eye.

I'd like to be able to say that lightning flashed, an angel appeared, or a small Earth tremor was felt at Cabell Huntington Hospital on the fourth of March in 1970, just prior to Billy's re-awakening. After all, that's what we'd like to believe—that God always heralds the miraculous with something spectacular. However, such was not the case. Billy simply stirred slightly, opened his eyes, and sat up. It was no more spectacular than that. Yes, God is still in the miracle business. But the business of miracles is not show-business. More often than not, God does miracles without a flourish and without any special effects. It's just as supernatural but it is not spectacular. Who would have guessed the spectacular was yet to come.

For a split second Aunt Pat thought she was seeing a ghost and nearly jumped out of her skin. Caught so completely off-guard, she uttered an involuntary, "Oh my God!" as she scrambled to her feet and rocketed to his bedside. Little Billy, weak and dazed, was sitting up and looking around the room with complete confusion on his face. Obviously bewildered at his surroundings, he gazed up at Pat with a blank stare for a second or two and raised his arms as though he wanted to be picked up.

Normally unflappable, Pat was momentarily beside herself as a million thoughts suddenly rushed through her mind: *Should I pick him up? Should I touch him? Will he try to get out of bed? Should I leave him and get a nurse?* Deciding on the latter course of action, she promptly rushed out into the hallway and shouted, "Nurse! Nurse! He's awake!" and just as promptly rushed back to his bed. A nurse appeared in a matter of seconds, and the circus began.

It would be no exaggeration to say that Billy's re-awakening that day caused a stir on the third floor of Cabell Huntington Hospital. As word spread among the hospital staff, his small room quickly became 'ground zero' as a steady procession of nurses, aides, candy-stripers, doctors, technicians, and even a janitor or two, made their way into and out of that room to see the miraculous—little Billy Anderson, the wonder-kid, fresh from death's door.

As the medical examinations began, it was soon apparent that something even more astounding had happened. Not only was Billy alert and fully conscious a mere six days after having his head literally crushed by a car's bumper, but he seemed perfectly fine.

Though naturally weak and stiff from six days of complete immobility, he did not display any ill-effects from the trauma or the surgery. The Man Upstairs, as Dr. Holbrook called Him, had outdone Himself—confounding and overturning the prognosis of the medical 'experts' in a startling and awesome display of miracle-working power.

Incredibly, in spite of the horrible injury and loss of brain tissue, there was no paralysis, no loss of mental function, no loss of motor skills, no seizures, and no visual or auditory problems. He didn't even seem to have any pain. In short, none of the *"permanent and irreversible"* things in Dr. Holbrook's report were evident and, frankly, he couldn't have been happier about it.

"Simply phenomenal, unbelievable," he said with unabashed joy after examining Billy. "I've seen a few unexplainable things as a physician, but this may be at the very top of the list."

As he would later admit to Mom and Dad, "Sometimes, it's simply wonderful to be wrong."

Joy Unspeakable

As they had done a dozen times in the last few days, Jim and Dorothy Anderson stepped out of the elevator on the third floor of Cabell Huntington Hospital and turned to walk down the long corridor to Billy's room. Running a little later than normal that evening, they both noticed an unusual flurry of activity at the other end of the hall.

As they drew nearer, they could see several people

walk into and out of what appeared to be Billy's room. Casting a quick sideways glance at each other, they quickened their pace. Within a few more steps, there was no doubt—Billy's room was the center of attention.

Grasping for each other's hand, they felt their hearts climb into their throats as they neared the door. Something was definitely going on in that room and the first awful thought that occurred to them was that Billy had died. Pausing momentarily, they entered, hand-in-hand, expecting the worst.

At first they couldn't decipher exactly what was happening. The room seemed to be wall-to-wall people, all of whom were clustered around the bed, cheerful and talkative. With so much chatter, no one seemed to notice them.

Aunt Pat, standing on the far side of the bed and facing the doorway, saw them first. "He's awake!" she shouted above the din, her face bursting into a radiant smile.

The other figures in the room, forming a near-solid wall around the bed, turned to see who she was speaking to and naturally stepped back. As the wall of people parted, their eyes fell upon the lone little figure lying in the bed, his dark eyes wide open. For the briefest of moments, Dad and Mom stood frozen in place, still not quite believing what their eyes told them. Then, in a twinkling, it hit home.

The room grew suddenly quiet. Quickly covering the few steps to Billy's bedside, they stood silently, wide-eyed and speechless, looking down at the most wondrous thing their eyes had ever beheld. No one said a word, instinctively knowing that this was one of those few moments in life best reserved for the majesty of silence.

Steadily gazing at their youngest son, and more importantly, having him look back, they realized the unrelenting nightmare of the last six days was mercifully over. As waves of elation and relief swept over them, Dad and Mom felt tears well up in their eyes and then roll down their cheeks.

It felt like a dream, almost unreal, almost too good to be true. From the depths of despair to the heights of unspeakable joy, the world suddenly and unexpectedly seemed right once more.

6

"I saw God..."

THEY SAY THE NEAREST feeling to pure joy that a human being can experience is the sudden cessation of agonizing pain. If that is true, then the second-nearest feeling must be the sudden cessation of great fear and anxiety—a feeling that Jim and Dorothy Anderson were privileged to know on the fourth evening of March in 1970. Later on that evening, I too was able to experience that most-joyous feeling, as were my brothers and sisters and, soon after, the rest of our extended family.

Surveillance Mode

That evening, as the sun was setting, I assumed "the position." The position I am referring to was a spot in our living room, in the center of the large picture window on the front of the house. Every evening for the last five days, I had taken up this position, as it afforded the best view of any vehicles approaching the house. I had entered surveillance mode, watching and waiting for any sign of the family station wagon.

I knew Dad would be home from the hospital soon and I was literally aching to hear the latest news about Billy. Unfortunately, the news had not really changed much since I began the ritual. Nevertheless, hope sprang eternal in the mind of a twelve-year-old boy, and I was once again in "the position."

This night, however, was especially troubling. Dad usually arrived home about seven-thirty and it was now nearly eight o'clock and I was starting to think something was wrong. Over the course of five evenings, I had grown adept at recognizing the headlights of our one family car. As soon as I knew the old station wagon was rolling up Kansas Street, I'd make a bee-line to the kitchen. There, I'd wait impatiently for Dad, all six-foot-three of him, to appear at the back door. Dad knew the routine too. Every night for the last five nights, he'd found me in the kitchen with the same earnest, probing look on my face. Even before he was through the door, I'd be asking, "How's Billy?"

This night was no different. As usual, I could feel my youthful pulse quicken as soon as I heard the car door close. As usual, the sound of his footsteps on the back stairs brought a nervous excitement I could feel all the way to my toes. As usual, before he was through the door, I blurted out the one question that had haunted me all that day and every day before.

But this night, instead of the usually quick answer —"He's about the same"—Dad paused and just smiled at me for a second or two. He knew I was dying to hear about Billy. He knew of the agony that I had borne over the last week. He also knew in just a few words I'd be feeling the same sweet release he himself had been enjoying for the last two hours, and he simply paused to savor the moment.

"Billy woke up today!" he finally said with a broad smile.

It was then that I noticed the look of sheer joy on my father's face, a look I had rarely seen before in my twelve years.

"He's AWAKE?" I shouted, not sure if I was dreaming.

"Yes, Jimmy, he's AWAKE!" Dad reiterated, playfully mocking my surprise and enjoying the chance to repeat the message.

I was instantly on cloud nine.

"Is he going to be okay?" I asked impatiently.

"Yes, it looks like he's going to be okay," came the happy reply.

My spirit soared. I was over the moon.

Words simply cannot describe what I felt at that moment. I've known times of intense joy in my life, but few if any, come close to the unfettered ecstasy I felt when Dad uttered those wonderful words. As the old saying goes, "It's better felt than tel't."

As I exploded in the kitchen, others in the house heard the commotion and came running. I don't think Dad had the privilege of telling anyone else that night. As soon as anyone came within earshot, I was exuberantly shouting the joyous news before he had a chance to say a word. Frankly, I don't think he cared in the least. I think he enjoyed watching his oldest son trumpet the good news more than he enjoyed telling it himself.

Dad did get a chance to spread the word by phone, and before long the street in front of our house looked like a parking lot as relatives near and far dropped by to enjoy the festivities. What a time we had that memorable night as the whole family shouted and laughed and danced and rejoiced at the news—little Billy Anderson was going to live, and on top of it all, he was going to be all right.

From all the noise we made, I'm sure half of Monroe Street got the message as well.

A Brady Bunch Moment

To say that Billy had none of Dr. Holbrook's predicted handicaps was true; to say that he was perfectly whole in every way and ready to come home, he was not. His head was still swollen and his face bore marks and bruises from the accident. He was weak and unsteady on his feet, and he needed time to recover from the surgery.

In addition, little Billy provided a living, breathing

case study for Dr. Holbrook and other interested physicians who wanted to observe his miraculous recovery to see if any quantifiable lessons could be learned with regard to head injuries. So, much to my dismay, Billy remained sequestered at Cabell Huntington Hospital for the time being.

Despite the fact that Billy did not seem to suffer from any impairments, there was one oddity that was noticed within the first few hours after he had regained consciousness. Simply put, he couldn't speak. Prior to the accident, Billy was a bonafide jabber-box with an excellent vocabulary for a five-year-old boy. Living in a boisterous house with seven talkative people apparently does wonders in conveying language skills. But since his awakening, he hadn't uttered a syllable, and in fact hadn't even tried.

Dr. Holbrook told my parents that speech is predominantly a function of the left hemisphere of the brain, and since the left side of Billy's brain had been directly injured in the accident, his inability to speak was not altogether unexpected—a condition known as *aphasia*.

"For the time being," he explained, "Billy will simple not be able to talk. However, sometimes the brain is able to compensate for this by shifting language function to a less-developed speech center on the right side of the brain. I've actually seen this happen in a few patients. So, whether this condition is temporary or permanent in Billy's case remains to be seen. We'll just have to wait."

Though not great news for my parents, at the time it

didn't seem to matter that much. Mute or not, we were just happy to have Billy back with us in any capacity.

For me, the next few days dragged by like cold molasses. Even though I knew he'd be all right, my twelve-year-old mind couldn't completely rest. Each day I wrestled with the same sort of aching frustration that Christmas Eve brings to every child, wanting so badly to see my little buddy again but knowing there wasn't a single thing I could do to speed things along.

I'm sure we all felt the same way about Billy, but for me—his big brother, his mentor, his protector—there was a special bond that made the whole ordeal a dozen times worse. Perhaps in my own mind, I felt a misplaced twinge of guilt that he had gotten hurt in the first place. In the logic of an adolescent boy, I may have thought that I should have been watching out for Billy a little more than I did the day of the accident, and was partly to blame. In any event, Billy simply couldn't get home soon enough for me.

I think Dad and Mom sensed the unusual strain I was still under and decided to give the whole family a treat. Piling in the old station wagon, we made our way up I-64 to Huntington that next Saturday to see Billy. Though hospital rules at the time prevented all of us from actually going to his room, they did not prevent us from standing on the hospital lawn. So, with the sun blazing brightly that afternoon, Ashland's version of the Brady Bunch gathered on the front lawn and looked up at Billy's third floor room as Mom carried him to the window in her arms.

It was the most beautiful sight I ever saw. He looked small and frail in her arms, with a huge white turban on his head. She held him at the window for just a few seconds, then took his wrist in her hand and waved it gently. We all waved back but I'm not sure he saw us in the glare of the sunlight.

She couldn't have stood there for more than thirty seconds before disappearing from view. No matter. However corny it might have seemed to those who passed by, it was just the right medicine at just the right time. We were all together again, however briefly, and it worked wonders on all of us.

Standing Room Only

Billy's remarkable recovery continued without any complications over the next several days. His accident and surgical wounds were healing nicely; he began eating normally; and his coordination slowly returned. Medical tests and evaluations revealed no detectable physical or mental abnormalities. His doctors continued to be astounded at what they were witnessing. The Great Physician was certainly putting on a clinic.

A few days later, Dr. Holbrook, finding no reasons to keep Billy in the hospital any longer, told my parents that he would be free to go home the following day. Dad and Mom gave us the good news at supper that night and a palpable mixture of excitement and anticipation settled over the

Anderson household.

How I exulted. Of course, at that point in time, I was still largely unaware of the true nature of Billy's injuries and the magnitude of his miraculous healing. Nor did I know that he had left this world three separate times on the operating table and returned. My parents, overwhelmed and overwrought as they were during the crisis, had not taken the time to explain the seriousness of Billy's condition to me or any of my brothers and sisters. I'm sure they reasoned that we were just too young to understand the details of it and, besides, there would be plenty of time for that later. Yet, even in my ignorance, the sense of relief and thankfulness I felt that night was overwhelming.

The following day, Wednesday, March 11, 1970, just thirteen days after his hideous head-crushing accident, little Billy Anderson was riding home in the front seat of the family station wagon, sitting between two of the seven happiest people on the face of the earth. The other five were waiting impatiently in Ashland.

Standing in the very same kitchen where I had experienced most of the highs and lows of the last two weeks, I remember his arrival vividly that bright, sunny day. He was carried up the back porch steps in my father's protective arms about 3:45 PM. Of course, it was standing-room-only in our little kitchen, as all of us were present and eager to welcome home the youngest member of the family with more than open arms.

He was still wearing that large turban-like bandage I'd seen from a distance the previous Saturday, and his eyes, somewhat dull-looking, had dark puffy circles under them. He had a rather blank look on his face as though he wasn't quite sure what was happening, and he didn't smile when he saw us. It was little Billy all right, but he seemed fragile, distant, and timid. I noticed right away that he was different, and at first it bothered me a great deal.

Although they had told us he couldn't talk, Dad and Mom hadn't really said what to expect. In my twelve-year-old mind, I had unconsciously thought that Billy would be more or less the same little boy he was before the accident. I was eager to resume our special big brother–little brother relationship and assumed we would just pick up where we left off.

But I quickly saw that wasn't going to be the case, and inwardly I found myself fretting that our relationship might not ever be that close again. But the joy of having him home quickly overrode my worries, and I determined, no matter the outcome, to be the best big brother I could be.

"I saw God..."

My parents had given us all strict instructions on how to act once Billy got home from the hospital. Since he was still recovering, we were not to be loud or rowdy when we were around him. Instead, we were to be on our best un-natural behavior and make sure he didn't fall or get jostled in any way. In a house full of rambunctious children, this wasn't going to be easy.

It was here that I rose to my former position. Unbeknownst to my parents and siblings, I silently anointed myself his special guardian and quietly stayed within eyeshot of Billy almost twenty-four hours a day. I was back in the saddle.

Over the next several days, the Anderson household gradually drifted back to normal. Billy settled in, got reacquainted with his siblings, and began to come out of his shell little by little. Dad and Mom encouraged us to include him in gentle play and to talk to him as much as possible. He and I would take short walks in the backyard, roll plastic Wiffle-balls back and forth to each other in our long downstairs hallway, and watch hour upon hour of cartoons.

Although he never spoke a single word, he would smile mischievously when watching the antics of *Tom and Jerry* or *The Three Stooges*, his favorite. He seemed to adjust quickly to his inability to speak and soon learned to nod his head 'yes' and 'no' and to point at whatever he wanted.

On the other side of the coin, having a mute member of the family was an odd yet enlightening experience for all of us. Somehow, in a way I can't fully explain, little Billy taught us the value of silence; that silence can sometimes be the perfect expression of love, and that we all tend to clutter our lives with words of little meaning. Or perhaps we all just talked a little less to make Billy feel more comfortable. In any event, the Anderson house was never quieter.

After we'd been shuffled off to bed, Billy would spend the evenings with Dad and Mom in our den. Sitting first on Dad's lap and then on Mom's, they'd watch TV. But mostly, I think they just wanted to feel the priceless enjoyment of holding Billy in their arms once again. After nearly losing him forever, it was sweet therapy for both. It was during one of these quiet evenings that the most unexpected and astonishing event in this entire drama took place.

Nothing seemed to be out of the ordinary that memorable evening. Billy had only been home a few days and, as usual, was sitting on Mom's lap. Dad was parked in his recliner after enjoying his turn with Billy. The TV was on. My parents had just finished a short conversation during a commercial when Billy, who was leaning back against Mom, sat up. Dad didn't notice. He sat there on her knee for a few seconds looking down at the floor, with a blank stare in his eyes, as though he was listening to something.

Then he turned and looked at my mother, and in clear, unmistakable words, *said*, "The doctors fixed my head...but God made me well...and I saw God...and Jesus is coming..."

Mom's jaw dropped. Dad jerked his head toward Mom and sat up straight. Both stared at Billy for a split second, mouths open, and then looked at each other in shock and disbelief.

Mom bent closer to Billy and peered intently into his face, not exactly sure what was happening. "What did you say?" she asked, incredulously.

Without blinking an eye, Billy calmly repeated his proclamation in the same short phrases, "The doctors fixed my head...but God made me well...and I saw God...and Jesus is coming..."

My parents sat in stunned silence. What in the world was happening here?

"Can you talk?" Mom asked, her voice almost rising to a shout.

Billy just looked at her for another second or two and then leaned back on Mom, assuming his original position. Nothing more was said. Just like that, it was over. Billy was not to speak another word for several weeks, until he gradually learned to talk all over again, like a small child would—word by word.

How could this be possible? For a brief instant, my youngest brother, recovering but quite unable to speak, made a startling, prophetic utterance and then fell silent once more until he learned to talk again months later. For a small boy who had rarely stepped inside a church building in all his five years, those few words were all the more staggering. How could he possibly have known of The Second Coming? Was this the result of his brief departure on the operating table?

Not being devout Christians at the time, these and other

questions haunted my parents afterward. As far as I know, they never told another living soul about this strange incident for many years. In fact, I was a young man in my mid-twenties when my father first told me of it. Mom later confirmed it to me in a separate conversation years later. Like my parents, I didn't know quite what to think of it. At the time, it seemed miraculous, supernatural—thoroughly unexplainable.

It wasn't until years later that I learned from the Bible that each person is composed of three separate parts: the spirit, the soul (or the mind), and the body (II Thessalonians 5:23; Deuteronomy 6:5). The words Billy spoke did not come from his mind, they came from his spirit.   According to the Word of God, all true prophetic utterances come from the Spirit of God through the spirit of man, not through the mind of man.

In this case, Billy's brain was still in the process of recovering, thus hindering the interaction between his mind and his vocal cords, but his spirit was untouched and free to express itself whenever he could get his tongue and his spirit in sync with one another. It apparently happened only once, but when it did it was breathtaking and awe-inspiring.

Little Billy Anderson apparently left this world briefly, just as Dr. Holbrook said, and made a short visit to Heaven where he saw God the Father and learned firsthand what the Bible teaches so eloquently—that Jesus will return to the earth someday. In just eighteen words, Billy confirmed that he died briefly; testified to The Source of his supernatural healing; and, if that weren't enough, validated the whole experience by proclaiming a Biblical truth he had no way of knowing.

"Yop"

Over the next several weeks, Billy's physical improvement continued on without any problems or setbacks. He made regular trips to Huntington to be examined by Dr. Holbrook and others, who were overjoyed at the progress he was making. Eventually, the surgery stitches, well over one hundred in number, were removed, leaving a meandering scar all the way around the left side of his head.

His coordination, appetite, and weight all returned to normal, and his outgoing disposition also began to resurface. In short, little Billy slowly but surely emerged from the grip of death, both literally and figuratively. Our close brotherly relationship, so important to me, was also restored in those first few weeks back home. Life was good.

Looking back, it was interesting to observe someone recovering from such a devastating head injury. Some aspects of normal living Billy quickly re-learned, and others were oddly difficult for him to comprehend. For example, it took him several months to consistently remember to tie his shoes when he put them on. Dressing himself, he had no problem with buttons, snaps, and zippers, but shoe laces apparently had no meaning to him. He would simply slip his shoes on in the morning and then go about his business with his laces untied, apparently oblivious and unconcerned about them, as though shoelaces had never been invented.

Of course, for someone recovering from brain surgery,

walking about with untied shoes is the equivalent of running with scissors. I remember Mom reacting with shrieks of horror the first time or two that Billy strolled into a room with his shoes untied. Before long, my parents realized that Billy had a 'blind-spot' in this area, and we were all put on high-alert about his shoes. I can't begin to number the times I saw my brothers and sisters tying or re-tying little Billy's shoes. Of course, eventually, he caught on, but for a while his mind simply could not comprehend the idea of shoelaces.

As expected, the one area of his recovery that was slowest in coming was his speech. Dr. Holbrook had warned us that Billy may not ever recover his ability to talk, but thankfully, over time, God restored that as well. Like an infant or a young toddler, he would pick up words one at a time and eventually began to string them together into short sentences. Like all young children learning to talk, there was plenty of humor along the way.

Once his verbal skills began to resurface, Mom and Dad would work with Billy in the evenings, re-introducing him to colors, numbers, and letters. These sessions were sometimes too funny for words. Occasionally Billy would fixate on a particular number, letter, or color. From that point on, sometimes for days, that number or color was Billy's answer to any question he was asked.

For instance, he once latched onto the color pink and for days on end everything in the entire world was pink. Mom might hand him a banana and ask him what color it was and he would answer—after several seconds of hard concentration—"pink." Stifling a smile, she would tell him that it was actually "yellow" and have Billy repeat the word "yellow" several times. Then she would ask him again what color the banana was and he'd answer with full confidence— "pink." It would have been very frustrating, and a little unnerving, if it hadn't been so drop-dead funny. You just couldn't help from laughing.

There was one single word that gave our little Billy more trouble than one could possibly imagine—the simple three-letter word "Y-E-S." For some inexplicable reason, Billy could simply not pronounce it. The first time he attempted to say "yes" it came out "yop." Apparently that first try imprinted itself upon his mind, and for months on end, "yes" always came out "yop."

Later, when he had developed a rather good vocabulary, "yop" would still escape his lips whenever he tried to say "yes." Even when he attempted to say it slowly and deliberately, it always came out "yop." It was the most comical thing you ever saw. Even Billy himself would burst out laughing in his vain attempts to master that devilish three-letter word.

Whenever Billy uttered one of his patented "yops," anyone within earshot would automatically reply, "Don't say 'yop'—say yes." As the weeks wore on, it became a game. Any time Billy let loose with a "yop," we would all pause, glance at one another, and then say in unison, "Don't say 'yop'—say yes." That little correction was uttered so many thousands of times during those months that the sentence has achieved folklore status in the Anderson household. To this day, there is no easier way to get a cheap laugh from one of my siblings than to say, without warning, "Don't say 'yop'—say yes." We all know instantly what it means, and it never fails to bring a smile.

At one point during the "yop" days, we despaired of Billy ever learning to say "yes" again. To preserve family harmony, we all, for a brief time, adopted the word as our own and said "yop" whenever we meant to say "yes." It made for some very interesting conversations.

When my father barely stopped himself from saying "yop" to his boss, he decided the fun was not worth the risk of public embarrassment and we were all wisely directed to drop the "yop." Thus, common sense prevailed, although "yop" still enjoys a mythical place in the official Anderson lexicon.

Incidentally, I am happy to report that Billy did eventually, after many months of relentless practice, learn to say "yes."

To God be the Glory!

7

Aftermath

AFTER LEAVING 66 FEET of skid marks in front of our house, Tom Carver Jr., who never personally contacted the family during the ordeal, quietly disappeared. However, I was later to learn that his father, Tom Carver, Sr., did stay in regular contact with my dad during that time, calling every few days for updates on Billy's condition and to discuss related insurance matters.

Far from being unconcerned, the Carver family, deeply troubled by the accident, chose to have Tom Sr. act as its sole representative and he in turn communicated only with my father. Dad, a man of few words himself, apparently never felt inclined to share that with anyone, leaving my mother with the mistaken notion that the Carver family was callous and indifferent to the accident.

Interestingly, Tom Carver Jr. was to meet my father in a most unusual coincidence seven months after the accident. Tom and his new wife were looking for an apartment to rent and answered a classified ad in the local newspaper. Calling the number, Tom spoke to a man with a deep voice, polite yet professional, who seemed eager to find a renter for the apartment.

At some point in the conversation, the voice on the other end said, "My name is Jim Anderson, what's yours?"

At that, Tom felt a sudden chill run down his spine, yet gathered his wits after a few seconds and bravely answered, "My name is…Tom Carver."

Then silence. For at least thirty tense seconds, there was nothing…but silence.

Then, suddenly, as though nothing had happened, the voice on the other end said, "I'd be happy to show you the apartment. When are you available?" Without a mention of the accident, they agreed to meet the following day.

In what was surely an awkward meeting, Tom and his new wife took a guided tour of the property with my dad but made no firm decision that day. Eventually, they agreed to terms and—seven months after the near-fatal accident— Tom Carver Jr. was living in one of the duplex apartments my father owned on 29th Street.

At no time during their initial meeting did either Dad or Tom bring up the accident. By that time, Billy was attending first grade at Oakview Elementary School and doing very well. It may have been that both men were simply content to let bygones be bygones, or perhaps it was just too fresh and uncomfortable for either to bring up. In any event, the matter was left untouched.

A few days after the Carvers moved in, Dad stopped by the apartment one evening to make sure all was well. At a pause in their conversation, Tom, prompted by his conscience, made a short but sincere apology for the accident. Again, he was met with silence. Not knowing what to say next, Tom let his words linger in the air.

Dad, obviously surprised and moved by the abrupt apology, stared at the floor for a few seconds and then simply nodded his head in response. Nothing else was said. My dad, ever stoic, accepted the apology but was simply unable or unwilling to talk about the near-loss of his youngest child with the man who was driving the car.

This is not to say that Dad bore a grudge or could not forgive Tom Carver. I think it is more than obvious by his renting the apartment to Tom that un-forgiveness was not an issue with my dad in this case. But my father, raised to believe that men did not show emotion, simply did not or could not bring himself to delve into matters that might bring his feelings to the surface, and simply chose to let the issue lie undisturbed.

The newly-wed Carvers lived in the apartment for four months and then moved elsewhere. Incredibly, Dad kept all these things to himself. Perhaps feeling that Mom would be too upset at the news, Dad never told her that Tom Carver— *the* Tom Carver—rented one of our duplex apartments during those few months.

To this day, Mom doesn't know.

Taking the Stand

As you might imagine, there were legal issues and major medical expenses to deal with after an accident of this magnitude. Dad and his attorney handled all of these arrangements with little involvement from anyone else in the family, including my mother. Although there was no citation issued to Tom Carver for traffic violations at the time of the accident, there were insurance claims to resolve.

Being one of the only eye-witnesses to the accident, I was asked to provide a deposition to help assist in sorting out these claims. Even as a twelve year old boy, I remember it well. One of the reasons I recall it vividly is because it occurred on a Saturday morning, greatly interfering with my Saturday morning cartoons. The other reason I remember it so well is because of a truth that I revealed during my testimony that changed my father's thoughts on the accident in general and of me in particular.

As we drove to an attorney's office that morning, I remember Dad telling me to answer all the questions I was going to be asked as completely and truthfully as I possibly could. I recall thinking how silly my dad's instructions seemed to me at the time. Was he actually thinking that I would try to hide the truth of what happened or invent something that didn't happen?

Later on, I realized that Dad knew from experience

that I was—as most twelve-year-old boys are—completely capable of massaging the truth when my scalp was on the line. Though Dad rarely bought my concoctions, he knew that I was both experienced and gifted in this area. Of course, it never would have occurred to me to shade the truth in a situation like this, but Dad wasn't taking any chances.

Seated around the biggest, smoothest, shiniest wooden table I'd ever seen in my life, a group of men in suits and ties hovered over me and began asking me a long series of questions. On the table in front of me was a microphone and, behind that, a very large and imposing reel-to-reel tape player. The men spoke in pleasant tones and I did my best to answer their questions, but the tape player intimidated me a little. Dad, sitting to my right, told me to ignore it as best I could and just answer their questions.

At one point in the proceedings, I was asked, "...And what caused you to be in the middle of the street when the car hit your brother Billy?"

Truthfully I answered, "Well, sir, I was going to get our football that had landed across the street in front of the Rothwell's house."

I noticed a puzzled look instantly appeared on my dad's face.

The man continued, "Your football?"

"Yes, we were playing football and the ball got loose and bounced across the street. I went to get it."

Casting a sideways glance, I could see that Dad was

visibly disturbed. Making a hand gesture, he signaled the group to stop the questioning momentarily. Someone reached over and pushed a button on the tape recorder, bringing those imposing reels to a smooth stop. I felt myself relax a little. The room grew suddenly quiet.

Dad thought for a second or two and then, leaning over very close to me, whispered, "I thought you were out there trying to rescue Billy?"

I just sat there with a look on my face that must have said, "What?"

"I always thought you ran into the street and tried to save Billy before the car could hit him. Didn't you?"

I remember the pleading look in my dad's eyes as though he desperately wanted that to be true.

"No, Dad...I was just chasing our football." I answered sheepishly, knowing that whatever I was saying was a blow to my father.

Dad just stared at me for a brief moment with a hint of sadness in his eyes. Then, recovering his dignity, he turned to the other men and nodded his head. The tape reels were put in motion again and the questions resumed.

Afterward, I realized that my dad had for months believed that his oldest son had risked his own life to try and save his little brother from certain death. Dad knew of the unusually close relationship Billy and I enjoyed and, unbeknownst to me, had assumed that I had acted heroically in the face of danger. To learn at the deposition that I was merely after a football was an obvious shock.

Though I never spoke to Dad about it, my mom told me years later that both she and Dad thought for months after the accident that I had risked my own life trying to save Billy. In some ways, I'm glad I didn't know that. Had I known the hero status I was accorded, I might have been tempted—at twelve years old—to believe it myself and to revise the truth of what happened to bring undeserved glory to myself. Still, in hindsight, it was disheartening to have to lower my parents' lofty opinion of me, even if it was in error.

The plain fact is that I was out in the street at the same time as Billy, not because I was heroic, but by sheer coincidence. That is, if you believe in coincidences. If, on the other hand, you believe the Hand of God was at work here, I will not argue with you. Frankly, I've never been able to make up my own mind on the subject. But I do know this—God did need *someone* to write this story...and I happened to be in the neighborhood at the time.

Settlement

Whether my deposition was very helpful or not, I'll never know. But, in time, a settlement was reached with Tom Carver's insurance company that awarded the Anderson family a total of $12,098.90. According to court documents, this money was to be used to cover all medical expenses and "for the support, maintenance and education of William David Anderson."

This amount would have been considerably higher had Billy been left with any permanent disabilities. As it was, his miraculous recovery kept the settlement figure relatively low. But no one seemed to mind. Given the choice, I'm sure we would have all preferred it *this* way.

It is more than interesting to note, in this day of skyrocketing medical expenses, the actual costs for all the medical services provided to Billy and myself as a result of the accident. If you can believe your eyes, the following is a summary of those costs:

Ambulance Service to KDH $18.00
Ambulance Service from KDH to CHH $25.00
Exam, X-rays, and Treatment at KDH (Jimmy) . . . $34.15
Exam, X-rays, and Treatment at KDH (Billy) $49.55
Surgery, ICU, Recovery & Rehab at CHH. $884.57
Exam, Surgery, EEG (Holbrook, Lobo, & Sakhia) . $915.00
Surgical Anesthesia (Brown, Haught, & Vega). . . . $90.00
Eye & Ear Exam and Testing (John Dole, MD). . . . $64.63

Total Medical Expenses $ 2,098.90

If you noticed, the settlement figure of $12,098.90 is a combination of the medical expenses plus an award of $10,000, a hefty sum in the early 1970s.

But what is so astonishing is that the costs listed above are absolutely paltry when compared to the astronomical prices we see for modern medical care. If my brother Billy would undergo the same procedures and the same hospitalization today, the estimated minimum total cost would be $200,000, or at least 100 times more expensive than in 1970.

Although most would agree that Americans enjoy the most advanced medical care in the world today, it has not come cheaply. The above example shows that costs have undergone roughly a 100-fold increase in just 40 years. To put that in perspective, the average cost for a new automobile in 1970 was $3,900. If prices for cars had kept pace with costs for medical care, we'd be paying an average of $390,000 for a new car today. Fortunately for us, no other sector of our economy has seen price increases anywhere near this magnitude.

Simply amazing.

The Hardest Head in Town

I'm happy to say that my brother Billy grew into adulthood without any complications from the accident. In fact, so complete was his healing that within just a few short years, the accident was nearly a forgotten chapter in the Anderson family. I say *nearly* forgotten, because Billy's battered head had the unfortunate tendency to be involved in several more accidents in the years after his initial head-crushing injury.

Despite all the precautions that my parents could impose on a young boy's activities, there was one thing they couldn't protect Billy from—himself. As unbelievable as it sounds, little Billy had two more serious head injuries before he reached the age of nine, causing Dad and Mom no end of frustration and worry.

The first occurred a little more than two years after the original car accident and involved—of all things—Dad's golf clubs. In his younger days, my father was an avid and excellent golfer, a lefty with a free and easy swing who excelled in long-distance drives off the tee. But earning a living for a fast-growing family left precious little time for play, and golf games on the weekends became fewer and fewer. By the time Billy was seven years old, Dad's clubs had gathered a thick layer of dust in the corner of our garage.

Enjoying the first few days of summer vacation in 1972, Billy and a neighborhood friend, John Bush, were puttering around our backyard looking for something to occupy their time and eventually wandered into the garage. There they found Dad's golf clubs, forlorn and friendless, begging for attention. Thinking they'd found just the right antidote to a rather boring afternoon, Billy and John selected a few of Dad's clubs, several wooden tees, and a handful of plastic golf balls, and headed to the vacant lot across the street for their first golf lesson.

I know it's hardly worth saying the obvious, but seven-year-old boys and golf clubs are a dangerous mixture. After several adventurous trips up and down the length of the lot, Billy and John had gotten rather good at hitting those tiny white balls. But the fun was soon to end.

Not realizing the operative word in "golf club" is "club," Billy absent-mindedly walked up behind John just as he decided to swing and—*whaaack!*—took the full force of a nine iron on the left side of his head. Struck just above his left temple, Billy crumpled instantly to the ground. Dazed but conscious, he got up slowly, blood streaming down his face, and took off for home, crying at the top of his lungs. Seven-year-old John Bush, thinking he'd killed his best friend, panicked and took off in the opposite direction. Once home, John sought refuge in a closet and—from his own account— spent the next four hours there, hiding from whatever dreadful news was sure to come.

Hearing Billy's screams before he got to our front door, Mom nearly went into hysterics when she first saw her youngest son. Still staggering from the blow, with blood pouring down the side of his face and head, Billy was a horrible sight to behold. Thankfully, Mom was able to calm herself enough to administer some quick first-aid and to find out from Billy what happened. After staunching the flow of blood from the deep gash on Billy's head, she phoned Dad at Beneficial Finance, and headed to the hospital.

In the end, Billy was found to have no skull fracture and no concussion. He did have an ugly jagged wound on the left side of his head that required a dozen stitches to close but, aside from that and the awful fright, he was basically fine. A few days after this episode, Dr. Holbrook ran another EEG on Billy just to make sure all was well and found no abnormalities, to the great relief of my parents.

They say that golf is a game of inches and it certainly proved to be true in this case. According to his doctors, had the golf club struck Billy's head an inch or two lower, in the temple area where the bone is relatively thin, he would likely not have survived the blow. Little Billy, with God's help, had dodged another close encounter with death by mere inches.

His second head injury occurred the following summer and, although it was certainly the least spectacular of all his accidents, it had very serious perils of its own. Unlike the golf-clubbing incident the previous year, this accident happened—if you can believe it—in the course of a card game. While I'll admit it's difficult, if not impossible, to think of card-playing as a dangerous activity, my brother Billy suffered a potentially fatal head injury while playing a children's card game called *Slap Jack*.

Unlike the previous two accidents, this one occurred in the safety and security of our backyard and was witnessed by my sister Kathy and my brother Bobby. Mom was also nearby but didn't actually see it happen.

Growing up, our large backyard was a haven for six rambunctious children. Surrounded by a fence, the landscape was formally divided into smaller areas by rows of bushes and shrubs. There was a detached garage with a covered patio, a concrete shuffleboard, a brick-and-mortar barbeque grill, and a very large above-ground swimming pool. A number of low-limbed maple trees dotted the property, just asking to be climbed. With so much space and so much to do, as kids, we could easily enjoy an entire fun-filled day without ever needing to leave our own backyard.

On this particular summer day, Mom had decided to scrub the patio and had removed the patio furniture, which consisted primarily of several folding lawn chairs and a large wooden picnic table. Asking Kathy and Bobby to help, they dragged the picnic table from the patio to spot on our shuffleboard. While Mom was busy hosing off the patio, Kathy, Bobby, and Billy sat down for an innocent game of *Slap Jack* on the picnic table.

Slap Jack is a very simple children's game in which the entire deck of cards is divided face-down among the players. The players take turns dealing cards from their hands onto a center pile of cards. The object is to be the first player to slap a Jack card when it appears face-up on the pile. Whoever slaps the Jack first acquires all the cards in the pile. The game continues in round-robin style until one player has accumulated all the cards.

Of course, to make the game fair, all players must have equal access to the center pile of cards. This can be difficult when three people are sitting at a picnic table with a bench on either side. To resolve the problem, Kathy and Bobby sat on the benches, opposite one another, and Billy, being the smallest, sat on top of the table itself. Unfortunately, no one noticed how close to the end of the table little Billy was sitting.

At some pivotal point in the game, Billy was able

to slap the next-appearing Jack on the pile and went into a spontaneous celebration. Throwing his hands up in the air and tossing his head back, he lost his balance and fell backward off the table onto the concrete, landing with considerable force on the back of his head. Screaming, both Kathy and Bobby jumped to their feet and ran to Billy's side. Mom, hearing a *thud* and the ensuing commotion, turned to see her youngest son lying motionless on the shuffleboard. Dropping her broom, she made a bee-line to little Billy, her heart pounding.

Kneeling beside him while trying to stifle involuntary tears, Mom was just about to gather him into her arms when Billy began to stir slightly and made a faint groan. Realizing that the next few minutes could be critical, Mom sent Bobby after her purse and car keys and instructed Kathy to call Dad at work and tell him to meet her, once again, at the emergency room.

By the time Bobby delivered her keys and purse, Billy had opened his eyes, but there was a distant, far-away look in them that spelled trouble. In addition, there was now an ugly purple knot growing on the back of his head. So, for the third time in four years, my mother found herself on the way to meet my father at King's Daughters Hospital with little Billy, the victim of yet another head injury.

Sitting in the emergency room together, Dad and Mom found themselves fighting the same anxiety that haunted them in 1970, and wondering if all the hard work of the last four years had been lost in this latest mishap. Fortunately, when the doctors emerged from their examination of Billy they had good news—no skull fracture or internal injuries, just a mild concussion and a painful bruise on the back of his head. With good nursing, he would be just fine in a week or so.

That same afternoon, my parents alerted Dr. Holbrook of Billy's most recent adventure and, two weeks later, took Billy to Huntington for yet another EEG. When the tests showed his brain wave patterns to be within normal limits, Dr. Holbrook could only shake his head in amazement, telling my relieved parents, "If another doctor had told me all of Billy's history—the accident and these other two injuries—and of his present normal condition, I'd be *very, very* hard pressed to believe him. All I can say for sure is this: Somebody up there really likes your little boy."

While I, too, am sure that the Hand of God was the single most vital element in keeping Billy through all these accidents, I wonder if something else may also have played a role. It's an old wives tale, but they say that a broken bone, once healed, is stronger than it was before the break. I've never been able to verify that, one way or another. But if it is true, then the original head-crushing accident in 1970 might have left Billy with a skull of much greater strength and density than normal, protecting him in some measure during the latter two accidents.

Do fractured bones actually grow back together stronger than before? Since doctors themselves disagree on the subject, I'm not sure we'll ever find a definitive answer. But if it is true, and

I suspect it is, then little Billy Anderson was sure to have—quite literally—the hardest head in town.

Fast Forward

Despite all the injuries to his head before the age of nine, Billy went on to live a thoroughly normal life, his teenage years mirroring those of myself and my siblings. A wonderful athlete, Billy played baseball, basketball and, surprisingly, given his head injury, football. A gifted runner, he set the all-time Ashland Elementary School 200-yard dash record just six years after the accident, a record that stands to this day.

After his recovery, Billy lost all conscious memories of the accident and his after-life experience. Even more incredible, he had no recollections at all of his life *before* the accident. It's as though his mental store of memories was completely erased and he started life all over again in a five-year-old body. Other than these missing memories, he seemed to be completely whole. To see him as an adult, you'd never begin to suspect he survived an accident of such horrific proportions. He is in every way a living, breathing miracle.

Yet little did anyone know that Bill's inability to recall even the slightest detail of the accident or his after-life experiences left an aching void in his life that haunted him mercilessly through the years. Like many who carry psychological wounds, he bore it silently. The "hole," as he described it, cast a long shadow on his life, gradually gaining intensity as he got older.

Whenever the accident came up in conversation, Bill would sometimes say how much he wished he could remember his experiences in Heaven. His comments never seemed like more than normal, natural curiosity. On those occasions, I'd sometimes mention that hypnosis might be a way for Bill to recover his "lost" memories, but it never went any further than that. Later, when Bill asked me to help him locate a good hypnotherapist, I should have sensed that something had changed.

Though he never said anything revealing, it later became obvious that Bill's natural curiosity grew into an unhealthy obsession that filled his mind with unanswerable questions. If hypnotherapy couldn't provide some relief, I was more than a little concerned that the "hole" might become a deep, dark pit from which my brother might never escape...

8

Heaven Revisited

April 5, 2010

"...NOW, BILL, I WOULD like you to go back in your mind to the day you were involved in a bad accident...at age five... go all the way back. Allow yourself to fall back in time before the first conversation you had with God...or Jesus. Are you there?"

"Yes," Bill said, in a soft, quiet voice.

"Okay. What do you see? Can you see anything?"

"There's a car..."

"There's a car?"

Bill suddenly began to stir, tossing his head from side to side, in obvious distress. His breathing became short and very labored.

Stephanie immediately took charge, "It's okay, Bill! It's okay! You're not there! You're here with us now...you're not there! Let it go! Just let all the fear go."

As if by command, Bill began to visibly relax and his

breathing slowly returned to normal.

Her soothing suggestions continued, "No need to remember that fear. No need at all. Let it go. Okay? You're safe and secure here now. Just let all the fear go."

Pausing a long moment to make sure Bill had fully relaxed, she began again, "Bill? What's happening now? What are you feeling?"

"Racing...my heart is racing."

"Your heart is racing? Is that because you are nervous or because you are excited?"

"I don't know."

"Can you see anything?"

Bill began to stir uncomfortably again, "HURT! I HURT!" Bill said, almost shouting. Tears appeared in the corners of his eyes and rolled down his cheeks.

Again, without hesitating, Stephanie stepped in, "We're not going to feel the hurt! Bill, let the hurt go! We're not interested in any pain. Relax and let the memory of the pain drift away, okay? You're not hurt. You're safe and secure. Just let all the pain go."

As before, Bill began to slowly calm down, his body movements relaxed and his breathing became normal.

"There you go...just relax. I want you to feel comfortable and completely at ease." After pausing for another moment to make sure everything had settled down, she asked, "Bill, are you completely relaxed now?"

"Yes," came the calm response.

"How are you feeling now? Is your heart still racing?"

"I'm fine...I was scared."

First Departure and Return

"So, where are you now, Bill? What can you see?"

"I'm in a bed."

"You're in a bed? Is there anyone there with you?"

"No."

"What do you see?"

"The angels," Bill said, still speaking in a quiet, almost child-like voice.

"How many angels are there?"

"Three."

"What are they doing? Do you know their names?"

Bill began to breathe deeply as though stirred by strong emotion, "A bright light!"

"A bright light...You see a bright light?"

Oblivious to the question, Bill suddenly shouted as if surprised, "I see sheeps!"

Grasping for understanding, Stephanie repeated Bill's words, "Sheeps? You see sheeps? What does that mean?"

It was at this moment that I realized the person answering Stephanie's questions was indeed a five-year-old boy. The soft, quiet voice I'd been hearing was not the usual strong voice of my adult brother Bill, it had the soft tenor of a small child. The word "sheeps" only confirmed what I had started to suspect. No adult would put an "s" on the end of "sheep." It was a mistake only a child would make. The realization stunned me.

"They're beautiful..." Bill continued. "They're in Heaven."

"Do you recognize them?"

"No, they're just...in a field."

"What does the field look like?"

"It's bright!" Bill answered, continuing to breathe deeply and excitedly. After another few seconds, "A rainbow!"

Pausing momentarily and trying desperately to understand what was happening, Stephanie asked, "Bill, do you see God?"

"Yes," he replied, his voice dripping with emotion and wonder.

"What does He look like?"

"A light!"

"Is there a message from God? Is He speaking to you?"

"You must go home."

"You must go home? Is that what God is saying to you?"

A look of dejection appeared on Bill's face. "Yes."

"And, home means here on Earth?"

Still breathing deeply and excitedly, "Yes...they say I must go...but I can't. Jesus said, 'Go back.'"

Stephanie Phelps, BA, CH

At these words, Stephanie turned and looked at me with wide eyes, as if to say, *Can you believe this?*

Bill continued on, speaking in a tender, pleading tone, "Why? Why?"

"Why? Are you asking the angels or Jesus?"

"Jesus."

"You're asking Jesus why you must go back? What does He say?"

"It's not my time…" Bill said, his voice trailing off in dejection. A look of overwhelming sadness now appeared on his face.

"Can you ask Him if there's a purpose in your going back?"

After a long pause, "My parents...need me."

"Will God or Jesus heal you now?"

"Yes...in time."

"In time?"

"Yes...I will be healed...in time." After another short pause, Bill continued, "...He is coming."

Startled, Stephanie asked, "What? Jesus is coming? When?"

"When it's right...yes."

"Is He saying anything else to you, Bill?"

"Go...back."

"Go back? Okay. Are the angels still with you?"

"Yes...they're beautiful...bright."

"Do you know their names?"

"No."

"Are they with you all the time?"

"They're always around me."

"Are they your Guardian Angels, then? Are these three angels your guardians in life?"

Speaking very softy, almost reverently, "Yes, they are..."

Bill suddenly began to stir uncomfortably, and his breathing became pronounced and labored as though in great pain.

Stephanie was quick to react, "You're fine, Bill!

You're fine! Breathe and relax! Just breathe and relax. What's happening, Bill?"

"I'm HURTING!" Bill shouts, his facial features twisted in a grimace.

"You're hurting? Let go of the pain!" she shouted, her voice matching Bill's in volume, "Let go of the pain! Just breathe and relax and let it drain from your body…just breathe and relax. Can you let it go?"

Almost instantly, Bill began to calm down again, his breathing slowed, and his facial expression softened as thought the pain was subsiding. Bill opened his eyes momentarily.

"Did the pain go away, Bill?" Stephanie asked. "Is it gone?"

"Yes."

"Good. Now, can you close your eyes again? Just relax and close your eyes. You're safe and secure."

"I'm okay…I'm calm."

Second Departure and Return

It seemed rather obvious, after this third upset, that Bill was subject to some distress whenever he was conscious of being in his body. Outside of his body, there were no problems, but apparently returning to an injured body was distressing to say the least. Hoping to avoid any further anguish, Stephanie waited quietly for a moment before resuming the session.

"Bill, are the angels around you now? Can you see them?"

"I see a light!"

"You see a light again? Where are you...can you tell?"

"...in a tunnel."

Surprised, she asked, "You're in a tunnel?"

"I'm flying."

"You're flying?"

By now, it was obvious to me that Stephanie was simply feeling her way through the session. Frequently, she'd repeat Bill's answers, not just to confirm what he said, but also, to give her a few seconds of time to formulate her next question. Being in un-chartered waters, it seemed like a perfectly natural thing to do.

"Are the angels with you? Are you moving toward the light?"

"It's bright!"

"It's bright...okay. Is there...?"

Before she could finish the question, a pained look appeared on Bill's face. "Don't go!" he shouted.

"Who do you not want to go?"

"The angels."

"Are they leaving you, Bill?"

With a great sigh of relief in his voice, "They're still here...they're going around me."

"Are you still in the light?"

"Yes...they say I must go."

"They say you must go from Heaven...back to Earth?

That you have to come back to the earth?"

"I don't want to..." he replied, his voice nearly breaking.

"Are the angels still around you, Bill?"

"No."

"Are you still in the light?"

Very quietly, he whispered, "It's dark..."

"Can you see at all? Can you tell where you are?"

"No...it's dark."

With that, Bill opened his eyes again and stared, unseeing, at the ceiling. Stirring slightly, he changed position as though uncomfortable.

"You're fine, Bill. Just relax and close your eyes."

As if on cue, Bill obeyed and quickly settled back into a gentle slumber, eyes closed, breathing calmly and evenly. Both Stephanie and I took the opportunity to stretch. It had been a long and intense forty-five minutes. Not wanting to break the spell, we didn't speak. After taking a moment to consult her notes, she gathered her thoughts and began the questioning again with renewed energy.

"Bill, where are you now? Can you see anything? Can you hear anything?"

"People...I hear people."

"Are you in the hospital?"

After a long pause, "Yes."

"What are the people saying? Can you tell?"

"They're touching me!" Bill said, with growing excitement. "They're touching me!"

"They're touching you?"

Bill's breathing accelerated again. "...my head! They're touching my head!"

"The doctors are touching your head?"

"Yes! I can feel them!"

"Are you in any pain? Does your head hurt?"

Bill's agitated breathing continued. "No...no pain."

"Are your angels around you? Can you see them anywhere?"

"They're in the room," he answered. Then pausing briefly, he added, excitedly, "I can see me!"

"You can see yourself?"

Bill suddenly became animated, lifting his arms off the bed and moving them wildly in the air above his body, hands outstretched, as though reaching for something unseen. Tossing his head from side to side, he shouted, "There's a bunch of them!"

Perplexed, Stephanie asked, "What? There's a bunch of what?"

Continuing his wild gyrations, Bill answered again with a shout, "ANGELS!"

"There's a bunch of angels around you? What are they doing?"

With joy and excitement, "I feel them! They're touching me!"

"Angels are touching you?"

"A bunch of them!" Bill said as his arms came slowly to a stop and fell back at his sides. His breathing returned to normal.

"Are they healing you?"

"They told me that."

Stephanie, wanting to slow down the pace of the session, recounted what had happened. "Okay. So, you're back in your body...in the hospital...and the angels tell you you're healed? Is that right?"

"Yes."

"So, your angels brought you back to your body?"

"Yes."

"How many times did the angels bring you back to your body?"

"Two," Bill replied, lifting two fingers on his left hand as he answered.

"Two? They brought you back to your body twice?"

At this, he lifted three fingers and said calmly, "Three times," apparently correcting himself.

Third Departure and Return

"And there are three angels with you each time you're out of your body?"

"Yes."

"Is Jesus with the angels each time?"

Bill grew silent. He seemed not to respond to Stephanie's question and after a long pause said excitedly, "I see a light!"

"A light...you see a light?"

Continuing to show wonder and exhilaration, "A BIG light!"

"Is it Jesus?"

"Yes!" he announced, his voice a mixture of joy and relief.

"What's He saying?"

There was no response. Bill lay there peacefully for some minutes, as though in a deep sleep. Stephanie, sensing that something unusual was going on, stopped the stream of questions, apparently deciding to let things happen naturally. I had the distinct impression that Bill was reliving the experience so intensely that it completely captured his attention, shutting him off from interacting with us.

After several more minutes, Bill said softly and with deep emotion, almost crying, "He loves me..."

"He loves you? Jesus said He loves you?"

"I have to go back..." Bill said, his voice again revealing the depth of his anguish.

"You have to go back? Does He say why?"

"No."

"Does He say anything else?"

"It's warm..."

Not quite grasping Bill's response, Stephanie repeated, "It's warm?"

"Yes."

"What's warm?"

When there was no response, she went back to her previous question, "Is Jesus saying anything else to you, Bill?"

"His hands are out...toward me."

"His hands are toward you? Is He saying anything?"

Bill's chest began to heave and after several deep breaths he replied, "He has healed me."

"He has healed you? Anything else?"

With a quiver in his voice, "He's not ready for me..."

"He's not ready for you?"

Dejectedly, "Not yet."

Bill suddenly began to move his head back and forth, as though looking desperately for something. "He's gone!"

"He's gone?"

Almost in a panic, "I don't want Him to go!"

"Are you sad when Jesus leaves?"

"Yes..." his voice trailing off in despair.

"How old are you, Bill?"

"I'm little...four or five."

"You're four or five?"

"Five."

Pausing a few seconds to gather her thoughts, Stephanie continued, "What do you see now? Can you tell where you're at?"

"There's a light."

"There's a light? What else do you see?"

Bill suddenly opened his eyes and lifted his head off the

pillow. Glassy-eyed, he looked around the room, disoriented. Then, just as suddenly, he lay back on the pillow again and closed his eyes.

"What did you see, Bill? Where are you at?"

After waiting a few seconds and getting no response, she asked again, "Bill, where are you at? Are you back in your body now?"

"Yes."

"Is the light gone now?"

"Yes."

"Is it dark?"

"No...I'm in a room."

"You're five years old and you're in a room...at the hospital?"

"Yes."

"Is anyone with you in the room?"

"Yes...Pat!" a note of surprise rings clearly in his voice. "I see Pat!"

"Is that Aunt Pat?"

"Yes!"

"What's Pat doing? Can you tell?"

After a brief pause, "I don't want a cookie!" he said, forcefully, as though talking to someone else.

Bill then opened his eyes and looked around the room again, seemingly more conscious than before. Sensing that he may be coming out of the trance, Stephanie reassured him, "It's okay, Bill. You're safe and secure. No need to be upset."

Without prompting, Bill closed his eyes again and lay back on the pillow, his breathing calm and regular.

"Can you go back to the hospital again, Bill?"

"Yes."

"So Aunt Pat offered you a cookie and you didn't want it?"

"No, I don't," he answered, tersely.

"Are your mom and dad there?"

"No…just Pat."

"Were you out of the coma then?"

"Yes."

"Are the angels there with you?"

"I can't see 'em," he replied, his voice rising playfully.

"You can't see them anymore? Are they just a memory now?"

Bill paused slightly as though thinking, then answered, "Just a memory."

"What are you doing now?"

"Resting…"

"You're resting?"

"Just…resting…"

Bill stirred slightly again, opened his eyes, and stared blankly at the ceiling, clearly beginning to come out of the hypnotic trance. Realizing that the session had run its natural course, Stephanie decided it was time to bring Bill back to full consciousness.

"Bill, I'm going to bring you out of trance now,

okay?"

"Okay."

"So now, on the count of five, you'll come back to the room feeling refreshed and relaxed and with full memory of the time you spent with Jesus and the angels, and with the complete healing of your physical body. So—ONE, the energy is coming back into your body now; TWO, you're feeling refreshed and relaxed; THREE, with lots and lots of energy; FOUR, bringing yourself back into the room, back into your body...and FIVE, eyes wide open...wide awake!"

To my utter astonishment, Bill's eyes popped wide open at the count of five, just like I'd seen it done on TV a dozen times. For some reason, I always thought that the waking of a hypnotized person on TV was pure showmanship, not the way it was really done in clinical settings with real professionals. Yet, when Stephanie uttered the magic word 'FIVE,' Bill opened his eyes like you'd shocked him awake with an electric cattle prod. I was dumbfounded. On top of all the amazing things we'd just heard over the last ninety minutes, this was the unexpected icing on the cake.

At that moment, I think if Stephanie had told me that Elvis was living in the attic, I might have believed her.

Afterglow

Bill lay in the day-bed a few more minutes, batting his eyes, and gathering his wits. Lifting his head and looking about, I wasn't sure he was altogether there.

"Are you back, Bill?" asked Stephanie.

"Uh-huh," Bill replied, sounding more like the Bill that drove up with me that morning.

"Are you back in the room?"

"Uh-huh."

"You did a great job. You did very, very well."

"Thank you...where am I?"

Stephanie and I chuckled at the question. Bill's eyes had that foggy, half-awake look in them, like most of his brain was still asleep.

"You're at The Counseling House in Parkersburg, West Virginia. Don't you remember?"

"Oh...yeah."

"Are you fully back with us now?"

"Yeah...I think so," came the drowsy reply.

Bill raised his arms above his head, stretching, and rolled his head in a circle as though loosening his neck muscles. A deep yawn escaped his lips. Rubbing his head, he sat up slowly, putting his feet on the floor and looking at me with a half-baked smile as though he couldn't quite figure out what I was doing in his bedroom.

"How do you feel?" Stephanie asked, eager to see if her client was no worse for the wear.

"I'm tired. I feel like I've been asleep all night long. I don't feel bad, just sleepy. My head hurts a little."

"Well, you were in trance for almost ninety minutes. It

can be tiring. Do you remember any of it?"

Staring at the floor for a moment, Bill's eyes slowly widened, as though a torrent of long-lost memories had suddenly come flooding into his conscious mind. The dawning realization seemed to snap him out of the doldrums.

"Yes...I remember...everything," he said, his excitement growing by the second. "Yes! I remember everything!"

Sitting on the side of the day-bed, it looked as if Bill was mentally rifling through a vault of new-found memories, and enjoying them like new toys on a Christmas morning.

"I remember seeing Jesus...I remember exactly what He looked like. I remember the angels...and the sheep...at least I think they were sheep. I remember Jesus saying I had to go back. I remember a rainbow..."

Each recollection seemed to spur him on to the next. Bill was on a roll, and neither Stephanie nor I felt like interrupting. Watching him, I had the impression that he was talking, not to us, but to himself, as though he was re-counting the whole experience to make sure it was real.

"I remember the car coming at me...I remember being in the hospital...and seeing Aunt Pat..." This went on for several minutes before he finally slowed down. Glancing at us, he declared, again, with a broad smile, "Yes, I remember everything!"

"Do you remember how many times you went to Heaven?" Stephanie asked.

"Two times, I think...maybe three. I'm not really sure."

That started Bill to thinking again. "I remember being in the tunnel...and angels touching me. I remember seeing Mom and Dad once..."

That startled me. "Hold it!" I said. "You remember seeing Mom and Dad?"

"Yeah."

"When was that? You never said so in the trance."

"I just remember seeing them for a split second when..."

"When you woke up?" I interrupted, finishing Bill's sentence for him.

"No...when I was in a coma."

"Oh, my goodness!" Stephanie exclaimed, obviously shocked.

"What?" I continued, in disbelief, "You were in the coma? How could you see them if you were in a coma?"

"I was like...coming up out of my body when I saw them," Bill answered.

"You were outside your body?"

"Yeah, I think I was going up, not coming back down. I remember seeing Mom and Dad, they were just standing there looking at me...like through a window. They were behind some glass, I think."

"That's right!" I nearly shouted, "I remember Mom telling me that you were in some sort of isolation unit the first night in the ICU and they could only stand there and look at you. What else do you remember?"

"I remember feeling so sad when I saw them because I knew I was leaving them. It broke my heart. I didn't want to leave."

"That's *so* amazing," I said, shaking my head. "I know that that must have happened, but I can hardly believe it. Can you still feel those emotions now?"

Dropping his eyes to the floor and pausing to reflect for a second, Bill answered, "No, not really. I remember feeling that way then, but not now. I feel just fine. I don't feel scared or sad or anything...I feel fine...really."

Recalling his periods of distress during the trance, I asked, rather gingerly, "So when you think of everything that happened to you, you don't feel any sort of emotional upset?"

"Nope."

Stephanie quickly added, "That's good, because there were a few times in the session when you were visibly upset and in some anguish. To me, it seemed like this always happened whenever you returned to your body. And we had to deal with that pain and have you release it. There were two things that probably combined to cause these episodes. First, it's likely that your body still carried cellular memories of being physically hurt at the age of five, and going back to the time of the accident naturally revived those memories. And the second element is something we call 'divine home-sickness'."

"Divine home-sickness?" I asked, making sure I heard her correctly.

"Yes. Divine home-sickness comes when you experience the incredible amount of love that Jesus holds for us. When you're in His presence, you're *so* close to Him—where you can almost touch Him—you feel this overwhelming love and you never want to leave it. So, if you're sent back to your body, you naturally yearn, with all your heart, to be back in that atmosphere of divine love. You know in a way that no one else does what it's like to be in that Light, and you long to go back and stay there."

"Divine home-sickness..." I repeated, turning the idea over in my mind. "...I'd never thought of that before."

Turning to Bill, I asked, "Do you think you feel anything like that?"

Standing to his feet and reaching for the ceiling with a grand stretch of his arms, Bill replied, laughing, "The only thing I'm feeling at the moment is a little dizzy...and a little hungry."

We all laughed and stood to our feet. It seemed our "little adventure" had come to an end. A few minutes later, we descended the winding staircase, slightly different people than when we went up. Pausing in the foyer of the old house before leaving, both Bill and I exchanged an affectionate hug with Stephanie. It just felt like the natural thing to do.

Filling in the 'Hole'

Driving back down I-77, I noticed Bill seemed unusually quiet as though he was still processing the incredible experience he'd just been through.

"How do you feel now?" I asked after an extended period of silence.

"Oh, I feel fine...very relaxed."

"Good...good," I said, wondering all the while what was really going on inside my younger brother.

"I feel...at peace," he volunteered, a few minutes later.

"So, you think the 'hole' in your life has been filled in?" I asked.

"I'm not sure exactly...not yet. Frankly, I don't know how I'm supposed to feel after something like that."

"You *are* glad we did this, right?"

"Oh yes, definitely. It's just...in some ways, it's more than I bargained for."

Bill rarely got philosophical, but the astonishing events of the day must have put him in an introspective mood.

"You know I always felt like something important was missing in my life and now I don't. Just like that..." he said, snapping his fingers, "I don't feel it anymore. It almost seems too easy, too simple. It's like I laid down in a bed and 90 minutes later I got up a different person. Do you have any idea what that's like?"

"You really feel *that* different?" I asked.

"Yeah, I do. It's like getting the answer to a life-long prayer when you really weren't expecting it. And now, I don't know exactly how to be...me. I'm going home a different person but I don't really know who this person is just yet. Isn't that weird?"

"I guess I never thought of it that way," I said. "But isn't that what you wanted?"

"Well, yes...I always wanted to be a different person—a better person. Before today, I couldn't be any different no matter how hard I tried, and now, all of the sudden, I'm different without trying at all."

Never articulate, Bill's well-spoken words caught me by surprise and left me wondering what other changes may have taken place in my brother that day. As the car grew quiet again, I found my mind drifting back to a phrase that Stephanie had used at the end of our session—"divine home-sickness." Somehow it kept echoing in my ears and as I turned it over in my mind, an idea began to form. After a few more minutes, a full-fledged theory had taken shape.

"Hey, Bill," I said, breaking the silence, "let me ask you a question."

"Okay."

"What do you think about 'divine home-sickness?' You know—the phrase Stephanie used there at the end, describing a person's desire to get back to heaven."

"I don't know...I hadn't really thought about it. Why

do you ask?"

"Well, I think I may know why you've felt like there was a 'hole' in your life for so many years, and I think it has to do with this idea of 'divine home-sickness'."

"Really?" Bill said, turning his head toward me and sitting up a little straighter. Glancing sideways, I could see a look of seriousness in Bill's eyes.

"What are you thinking, Jim?"

Pausing a few seconds to put my jumbled thoughts into some coherent form, I began, "If you remember, Stephanie said people that have actually been to Heaven or been in the presence of Jesus have an understandably intense desire to go back there, right?"

"Right."

"Well, maybe the mental distress you've felt through the years was due to a disconnection between your mind and your spirit. You see—your spirit longed to go back to Heaven and that desire naturally produced strong feelings. But because your conscious mind had lost the memories of that experience, you had no way of knowing why you had these strong feelings, where they were coming from, or how to turn them off. So that set up a conflict on the inside of you. Does that make sense?"

"I guess so…sort of."

"In other words, for all these years you've been feeling this intense desire for something that your mind could not identify with. This desire was coming from your spirit, but your mind couldn't begin to grasp it because it had lost its memories of your visits to Heaven. In your mind, there was no reason to feel this way, yet these powerful, mysterious feelings were there—undeniable and irresistible."

"I think I see what you're saying."

"And, as you got older, the intensity of these feelings increased, leaving you more than ever in the dark as to what they were and where they were coming from."

"You're saying...my spirit and my mind were at odds because my spirit knew something my mind didn't know?"

"Yes—exactly! And something your mind *couldn't* know...until those memories were restored. See what I'm saying?"

"I think so. It's starting to make sense to me now."

"Actually, I think it's more correct to say your spirit and your mind were at odds because your spirit remembered something your mind had forgotten. That in turn produced an inner conflict and that conflict could only end if those memories were restored to your conscious mind. Once these memories were restored, then your mind and spirit would be in tune with one another and the turmoil could cease. At least, that's what I'm thinking."

"You're saying, as soon as my mind understood what and why I was feeling this way the inner conflict would cease?"

"Yes."

"So...the turmoil was really due to the fact that I didn't

know why I was feeling these feelings, right?"

"Right. And today those memories were restored to your mind. So from now on, whenever you experience this deep, longing sensation that used to drive you crazy, you'll know what it is and why you feel that way. I would think that the restoration of your heavenly memories has now officially and permanently filled in the 'hole' in your life."

Suddenly not sure that my off-the-cuff analysis rang true or not, I quickly added, "Or is this total nonsense?"

Bill just sat there for a long minute, staring straight ahead and not saying a word, apparently lost in deep thought. Happy that I was able to communicate these unorthodox thoughts to Bill in an understandable way, I thought it best to let the theory sink in without further comment.

Finally, Bill said in a low, quiet voice, "Wow...it all makes total sense now. I don't see how you could possibly be wrong. That's got to be it."

Wanting to make my case as convincing as possible, I added, "After all, didn't you just say you felt 'at peace?' From what you've told me, isn't that a huge change from the way you've felt in recent years? Even from the way you felt this morning?"

"Absolutely."

"Well then, it sounds to me like the war is over—your mind and your spirit are finally in harmony."

"Yes...I do feel completely different."

"And how would you describe—in one sentence—

how you feel?"

After a thoughtful few seconds, Bill smiled and replied, "It's like a gentle calm… after a long storm."

Relieved that we might have finally put the issue to rest, I glanced at Bill and winked, "No charge, brother…it's on the house."

Feeling like we'd exhausted the subject for the time being and wanting to relax a little, the conversation turned to lighter topics and we passed the time, as we usually did, reminiscing about our younger days. Later, as we neared the Kentucky border, Bill brought up the day's adventure yet again.

"I'll tell you something else that's strange, Jim."

"What's that?" I asked.

"You know I got saved years ago, but as strange as it sounds, I really feel like I just got born again…again. Spiritual things are suddenly so real and it makes me feel different… very, very different."

"Well," I said, thinking out loud, "I wouldn't over-analyze it if I were you. What you experienced today has changed your reality, and it will take you some time to adjust to this new reality. Nothing on the outside of you has changed—the change is on the inside. You're just feeling different because you have a new internal awareness you didn't have before and that new awareness is altering your perception of reality. That's what you're feeling. You *feel* different because you *are* different."

"Yes...I guess I am."

"Think about it—you got to revisit Heaven today. You can't have an experience like that and *not* be different afterward. But I wouldn't worry about it...just relax and let things happen naturally. You'll be fine."

"I'm sure you're right. I'm just a little unsure of myself, that's all. I feel like there's a whole new Bill Anderson to discover."

I couldn't resist the opening, "Well, let's hope so. Everyone was pretty fed up with the old Bill. Everyone was hoping I'd come back with a new one."

We both laughed.

As the miles flew by, Bill grew quiet again, immersed in his own thoughts.

After several minutes, I touched lightly on the subject again, "Well, looks like you were right this morning—we've been on quite a 'little adventure' today, haven't we?"

Bill glanced at me, with a happy smile. "Yeah, it's been more than wonderful, but I feel like the *real* adventure is just beginning..."

9

Heaven Revealed: An In-Depth Interview

DIFFERENT PEOPLE HAVE DIFFERENT ideas of life beyond the grave, but there are few not interested in the matter. It is said that two thousand books have been written on this subject. Almost any book that tries to tell us about it finds ready purchasers. I suppose one reason for this is that people are apt to be more interested in what is coming next than they are in the present. Some have asked, 'Why do we not know more about what is to be hereafter?' Perhaps it is best that much of it should be kept from us. I fear that if we knew all, we would lose interest in the present and so waste its opportunities.

—David C. Cook, *Intra Muros*

Beyond the Veil

Stories of life-after-death experiences have always held a deep fascination for me. After all, what's more important to any person than their own life? If we live beyond the death of our bodies, is there any issue larger than the eternal destiny of our souls? I would say not.

Many have said through the years that the only certainties in life are death and taxes. That may be true, but the study of taxes has never claimed my attention like the study of life after death. It is the penultimate question of human existence, the inescapable fate of all human beings. To get a glimpse of what lies beyond our own mortality is, therefore, an irresistible subject to me, as it is to most people.

I'm sure my heightened interest in Near-Death Experiences (NDE) was born in the drama surrounding Billy's accident in 1970. It was likely the single most formative experience of my young life and as such it acted as a catalyst to intensify my own natural interest in the topic. From boyhood on, I've always been awestruck to read the experiences of those who have slipped "beyond the veil" and returned. The same holds true today.

Through the years, I've found it is a curious field of study—fraught with many things unknown and unknowable. It is not a "science" in the strictest sense of the word, although the science of medicine has given us an ever-widening window into this most-captivating of subjects. Modern resuscitation methods have greatly increased the chances for individuals to step briefly beyond death's door and to return, giving rise to a veritable explosion of NDEs in recent decades.

Many hundreds, even thousands, have had such

experiences, and one of the remarkable characteristics of these episodes is that they vary widely from person to person. Almost no two experiences are alike. Some are good and some are horrific; some are pleasant, some are terrifying. While there are some general features of NDEs that seem to be somewhat common, such as seeing Jesus or various spirit beings (angels, demons), traveling through a tunnel, meeting departed relatives, etc., each occurrence is utterly unique to that individual.

It's as though each person does indeed have their own separate and distinct destiny awaiting them and no amount of study and conjecture can lay out all the details ahead of time. Much remains a mystery, as it is apparently intended to be. The Apostle Paul wrote, quoting the Prophet Isaiah, "But as it is written, Eye hath not seen, nor ear heard, neither have entered into the heart of man, the things which God hath prepared for them that love him." (I Cor. 2:9) Jesus Himself said, "If I have told you earthly things, and ye believe not, how shall ye believe, if I tell you of heavenly things?" (John 3:12)

Thus, it seems that the Lord has shielded us from knowledge of the hereafter by a "curtain of ambiguity" that is both impenetrable and entirely intentional. That being the case, each NDE should be considered just a temporary "glimpse" of what awaits us, and not a full-fledged drawing away of the curtain. That is apparently reserved only for those who have permanently departed.

Of course, this ambiguity is quite frustrating to those of us on this side of the curtain. Man always seeks to order his thinking. He has learned through the millennia that understanding any subject depends on discovering the organizing laws and principles that govern that subject. NDEs are the epitome of a field of study that seems to have no recognizable structure or order. The wildly varying experiences from person to person seem to defy any neat and orderly understanding of life in the hereafter. Beyond the general division of Heaven and Hell, it all seems relatively unpredictable, and man instinctively dislikes that which he cannot grasp in a rational or logical manner.

The randomness that characterizes NDEs leads some to question their validity. This group of cynics also includes those who insist that the soul does not survive the death of the body but perishes with it. Those who hold such views believe that any supposed experiences outside the body are merely the result of drug-induced hallucinations, the disorganized firings of human brain cells at the point of death, or a combination of similar factors. Further, they believe that what others claim as genuine out-of-body experiences are just dreamlike illusions based on social and religious conditioning.

For example, skeptics would say that those who report being ushered into the presence of Jesus by angels or entering a dark, foreboding area where other souls are in torment are not experiencing any such thing, but are simply having a fanciful dream, or nightmare, based on their pre-conditioned ideas. To those who hold these opinions, no single NDE is persuasive, and no amount of evidence to the contrary will convince them that out-of-body experiences are real and genuine.

I point this out only to make the case that my brother Billy's experience seems to fall outside of the realm where much honest skepticism could be leveled. To begin with, the vast majority of NDEs occur to adults, rather than to children. Documented out-of-body experiences in young children, ages five and under, are extremely rare in comparison to the number of adult NDEs. Consequently, the social, cultural, and religious conditioning which might play a role in adult NDEs would be a non-factor in the experiences of most very young children.

This would certainly be true in Billy's case, as he was not a child who spent time in Church. As I mentioned earlier, we were at best an extremely sporadic church-going family, which means that little Billy was not exposed to formal "religious" training during his early years. This fact makes his earlier proclamation after returning home from the hospital and his subsequent revelations during hypnosis all the more believable. Simply put, Billy was not pre-conditioned to believe in spiritual things and would certainly not have gleaned this information from the home he lived in.

Secondly, though Billy was terribly injured, he had not been given any narcotics or other drugs which would have induced some type of hallucinogenic dream. He certainly was receiving emergency medical attention, but that attention was for the purpose of stabilizing his physical condition, not dealing with pain or other related symptoms. After all, he was completely unconscious from the moment of the injury, eliminating any real need to deal with pain. From what can be known, Billy's episodes of leaving his body occurred in the emergency room or during pre-op, and the only things likely administered there were infusions of saline and blood plasma. Again, the facts here tend to puncture any suggestion that Billy's experience was generated or influenced by heavy doses of drugs.

In sum, from what information can be gathered, the entirety of Billy's experience is a rarity that does not fall neatly into normal NDE categories. His age, his lack of religious training, and the conditions surrounding events in the hospital are factors that combine to virtually eliminate all of the various arguments put forth to cast doubt on the authenticity of NDEs. What I am suggesting here is that my brother's experience is one of those rare instances where the believability of his NDE is nearly unassailable.

Further, it seems that events on both sides of the "curtain of ambiguity" coincide perfectly. That is, all the statements from Bill, both after the accident and during hypnosis, harmonize in every way with what is known to have occurred on this side of the curtain. Thus, not only are the arguments from skeptics found not to apply in this case, but all of the facts that can be garnered support and corroborate one another.

All things considered, I would contend that my brother Bill's NDE is one of those rare and remarkable instances where the authenticity of the event cannot be explained away, but should be understood and embraced as a genuine glimpse into the spirit world. His supernatural experience confirms that the human spirit does indeed survive the death of the body and that the hereafter is as the Bible describes it.

Questions and Answers — An In-Depth Interview

During the hypnotic session with Stephanie, it became obvious early on that the person she was conversing with was a small child. The change in voice tone, the limited vocabulary, and the response to various questions all indicated she was interacting with someone very young. The "age regression" technique she employed apparently worked very well in Bill's case, taking him back to the tender age of five.

Going back to that age was of course necessary to gain access to the events surrounding the accident. But there were obvious limitations as to what could be learned. A five-year-old boy would simply not have the maturity or the vocabulary to adequately describe what he was seeing and experiencing. Thankfully, the memories of Billy's NDE were restored to his conscious mind during the session and were fully accessible once he awoke.

Today, Bill can recall with clarity all of the events that happened to him after the accident, making it possible to delve deeply into everything he experienced on the other side of the "curtain." That being the case, I conducted an in-depth interview with Bill just six days after our trip to the Counseling House in Parkersburg, WV. The following is a transcript of that question-and-answer session.

*   *   *   *

Before the hypnosis, you had absolutely no recollection of the accident or afterward?

No, not at all. I have just the vaguest recollection of being in the alley behind our house on the day of the accident.

And after you awoke from the hypnotherapy session, you had no memory of the previous 90 minutes?

No, it just seemed like I'd been asleep all day. My eyes felt heavy and my head hurt a little—like I'd slept too long. I didn't know where I was at first and it took me a minute or two to get oriented; then I remembered where I was…pretty strange experience, actually.

When you woke up, did it seem like you'd been dreaming?

It's hard to explain, but no, I didn't have any recollections of the session at all and it didn't seem like I'd had a dream.

I just woke up and suddenly there was a whole new set of memories in my mind that weren't there before. They just seemed like ordinary memories, not like a dream...and it seemed like I had lived these experiences. They were now just normal memories—like I'd remembered something that happened to me as a kid.

So these lost memories were in fact restored in your mind?

Oh yes. I can remember it just like any other memory now.

So what's your first recollection of the accident—the car?

I remember a car. I don't know much else. I just saw it—just a fleeting glimpse of a car coming at me. It seemed dark in color in my mind. I don't see it like it's on a movie screen—like I'm watching myself—but more like I'm actually living it. I'm a little boy out in the street and it's coming at me...but it doesn't scare me.

So you actually saw the car before it hit you? I thought you never saw it.

Oh, I saw it just for a split second, and was trying to get out of the way. But I don't remember it hitting me. The whole thing is just a short blip in my memory. I think I saw it after I'd started across the street but it was too late to stop in time, so I speeded up to get out of the way. I didn't think it would hit me.

And the memory of it doesn't bother you now?

No, it doesn't bother me.

The reason I ask is because there were times during the session when you seemed to be in distress or scared and Stephanie would have to calm you down. Do you recall anything like that?

I have no memory of that at all.

Do you have two or three separate recollections of being in Heaven, or is it all one experience in your memory?

I seem to remember two separate visits and another very short one.

Can you tell us about the first visit?

I'm not exactly sure which one was first. I remember going through a tunnel twice, once each time. I think the first visit I remember most. It might have lasted the longest, but I don't know for sure. I remember seeing Jesus and I remember exactly what He looked like. I remember the figure, the hair, the beard, the face. I saw the lights of Heaven, the angels, and all sorts of wonderful sights. It was hard to take it all in.

So you remember going into a tunnel and coming back through a tunnel?

Yes. I remember going probably a little more than coming back. I remember whenever I'd come back through, it was dark at the end of the tunnel. It was dark and I couldn't see anything. It's like whenever I'd come back to my body it was dark, like my eyes were closed. Then I'd realize I'm in a room.

What was the tunnel like—was there a light at the end of the tunnel? A feeling of speed as you went through it?

It was odd. I don't remember feeling like I was speeding through it but there was a mild sensation that I was flying. There was a light at the end of the tunnel like it opened up into another place or another world. When I got to the end, it seemed like my vision expanded and I could see out the end of the tunnel into this bright place. It looked like paradise to me.

Did you see the tunnel walls? Why did you think it was a tunnel?

You just had the sensation of moving through a tunnel is all I can say. It was just like going through a tunnel on Earth. There was a light at the end and it kept getting bigger and bigger.

Did you see angels in the tunnel?

I want to say I knew they were around me, but they weren't in front of me where I could see them. But they seemed to be going with me, or carrying me through the tunnel. They seemed to be my escorts.

Did you know where you were going when you were moving through the tunnel?

Yes, I did. I know that sounds odd, but I just had the feeling or the knowledge that I was going to Heaven. Somehow I just knew it and it was a very calm, peaceful, pleasant type of feeling. I wasn't scared at all. I knew where I was going and it felt like I was drawn or carried there by some unseen force. Thinking about it now, there was just a sense that something very good was ahead of me.

Was Jesus at the end of the tunnel? What did you see?

No, He wasn't there at first. I just remember seeing this very wonderful place. It looked like a beautiful, perfectly-manicured park with green grass and flowers...gorgeous colors everywhere, but no people. There were animals there and the sky was a rainbow. I don't mean I saw a rainbow in the sky, I mean the entire sky was a rainbow. It was SO beautiful! Except for the sky, it reminded me of Earth, but much, much better. It was perfect in every way.

Did you exit the tunnel and come out into this area?

I seemed more like I was looking out the end of the tunnel but not actually standing in this place.

Tell me about the animals you saw...

Well, to me, they looked like sheep, although they might have been something else. They were in a bright, green, grassy field in front of a hill that sloped upward. They weren't real close to me. There were about fifty of them, I guess. They were very beautiful and white as I recall. I don't remember if they were doing anything specific, like eating grass. They were just there moving around. I didn't see any other kind of animal and no people. I don't remember seeing any trees in this place, but there were yellow flowers scattered all around the field and the hillside. I don't know what it means, if anything. I just know I saw them and at first it surprised me.

Why did it surprise you?

Well, I knew I was going to Heaven when I was in the tunnel

and as I approached the light and got to the end, it just surprised me that the first thing I saw was sheep, and not Jesus or other people. When I think about it, it still sort of surprises me.

What happened next? Did Jesus appear in this place?

I don't think so. It seems like I was taken to another place. How, I don't know. When I first saw Jesus, it wasn't in this setting. It seemed like another area. I didn't see anyone else, just Jesus, and it seemed like we were outside in an area with mountains. It was just as beautiful as the green meadow, but it was mountainous. These weren't huge snow-covered mountains like the Alps or the Himalayas. They were very steep, tree-covered slopes like you'd see in the Smokey Mountains or the Blue Ridge Mountains. I remember there were three peaks I could see behind Jesus. The sky was not a rainbow here but a deep, gorgeous blue color with white clouds, very much like Earth. The atmosphere seemed crisp and clear like it was early morning. And there were angels around me and around Him in this place…they were everywhere.

When you first saw Jesus did you know who He was?

Oh yes…instantly. I don't know how but there was no doubt whatsoever who He was when I saw Him. He's quite unmistakable. He doesn't need a name tag. *(laughs)*

What did Jesus look like? Can you remember details?

Yes and no. He didn't look like anyone I could compare him to on Earth. He looked like nobody I'd ever seen before. He was good-looking. Not movie-star good-looks, like Cary Grant or Dean Martin or Tom Selleck, but very attractive. He didn't remind me of anyone. Somehow He didn't quite look like a normal human person. It was His Presence! His Presence just overwhelms you and that's all you really feel and notice—not so much what he looks like or how tall He is, you are just captured by this intense feeling of love and joy. I don't really know how to describe it. He's surrounded by this power and glory and you FEEL it! It's just overpowering. It does something to you and you just want to fall on your knees and stay there.

What else did you notice about Him?

Well, I never really noticed or saw His body so much. I could see His face but it was like His body or His robe were made of light and you couldn't really see it. It seems like this light formed a mist around Him and you couldn't see Him as distinctly as you see a normal person. He was just surrounded by this Glory and it shown out from His body or His robe.

Can you describe anything else about His appearance?

He had a full beard and a full head of long wavy hair, not curly, but wavy, more or less like you see Him in pictures. His hair was about shoulder-length, covering his ears, maybe longer in the back. It was dark, as were his eyes. Funny, his hair seemed to be in constant motion, like it was being gently blown by the wind. I had an impression of great age, not that He looked old, but that He was ageless, like He'd been alive forever. He seemed big to me, like an adult, but I think that's because I was only five at the time this happened. It's an unforgettable image…I'll never forget it.

So when you were in Heaven, you had the impression you were a small child?

Oh yes. Jesus was taller than I was and I remember looking up at Him as He spoke. In my memory, I'm definitely little—a small child.

What about His robe—was there anything you noticed?

His robe seemed almost alive. It wasn't some heavy material that just hung on Him. It was light and sheer and flowed around Him. Like His hair, it was in constant motion, like being blown in the wind, and it glowed with light. I mostly saw the upper part of Him because all of your focus is on His face, so you really don't notice the rest of His body.

Can you tell me about your conversation with Him the first time?

He just suddenly appeared in front of me in this beautiful mountainous setting after I'd seen the sheep in the field. And He told me that it was not my time to come and that I had to go back...nothing more that I recall. It was a short conversation. I remember the awful feeling when he told me I had to go back. I remember pleading, "Why? Why?" because I DIDN'T want to go back. I definitely remember that! Then He told me, again, that it was not my time. I remember how I felt at the moment—like I was exactly in the right place. It was warm and peaceful and I felt completely secure and loved. It was like a fantasy world where every need and every feeling you could ever desire was right there at your fingertips. You were just surrounded by perfection in every possible way, and the thought of leaving was almost terrifying. It was awful... awful.

During the session, you mentioned another reason that Jesus was sending you back to Earth—do you remember what it was?

Yes...my parents. I mostly remember Him saying it wasn't my time but I have a faint memory or impression that He spoke of my parents and that my going back also had to do with them. It was for their benefit. But this is just a faint recollection. I mostly recall Him telling me it wasn't my time.

Did you ever see God Himself?

Well—*now*—I don't think I did. I know I saw Jesus and the angels but I don't remember seeing anyone else or any other being. I was told I said to Mom and Dad that "I saw God" but—at five years old—maybe I couldn't or didn't distinguish between God and Jesus. In other words, maybe at that time I thought they were the same. I guess I can't really say for sure but in my new memories I only remember seeing Jesus, not God.

Did you see any other persons? Any relatives?

No.

Were there angels around when you spoke to Jesus?

There were always angels around. All through the whole experience, angels were always around me. I was never alone.

What did the angels look like?

Well, I never could see them distinctly. There were usually at least three that stayed in my field of vision, in front of me. They were small, like me, and they glowed such that you couldn't see their faces. In my mind, they were sort of like ghosts, actually. I didn't see any wings but their clothes were bright, loose, and flowing, always moving. They were indistinct enough that I couldn't tell if they were male or female. They were just beings made of what appeared to be white light, all the same size, with no real distinctions between the three. I don't know how but I knew instantly that they were angels and I was never afraid, but felt safe and secure in their presence. One thing especially that I remember is that the ones I saw were small and seemed child-like in a lot of ways. At least it seemed that way to me. It surprised me. They weren't adult size, they were my size or just a little bigger.

So these three angels were similar yet different?

They weren't carbon copies of each other; you could tell they were three different beings, although I never saw their faces clearly. They were very similar though. They were human-like. As I said, I couldn't see any wings because their clothes or robes were always moving and flowing, sort of obscuring my view of them. Because they were bright and glowing and they seemed to always be in motion, they were somewhat ghostly in appearance, but I could tell they had long hair, similar to Jesus. I remember that they had no beards, and looked very young.

Do you recall any other details about the angels? They didn't speak to you at all?

No, they never spoke, but they were always around me. They didn't talk to each other that I know of but they all seemed to have the same purpose, and they worked together to escort me here or there and to protect me. They seemed to know what I was thinking and I never felt scared or afraid of them, even though they were very different from anything I'd ever seen before. There might have been some sort of non-spoken communication between them because they all worked together smoothly and cooperatively. I remember that whenever I'd leave my body, they'd be right there to pull me upward and set me moving toward Heaven.

How would you describe the light around Jesus and the angels?

It was white and very bright, but not blinding. The light around Jesus was infinitely more bright and spectacular than the light around the angels. I remember feeling a warmth but I don't know if it came from the light or not. It was just beautiful to see.

Anything else you remember about Heaven?

Music…I remember hearing music in the air. It was a different kind of music that I can't begin to describe. There wasn't any vocals or voices singing, just this beautiful, soft, melodic music all around. It was similar to orchestral music but it had a lot of bell sounds, or bell-like sounds, in it. I don't know where it came from but it was all around in the atmosphere. Like everything there, it almost seemed to be alive. It's hard to explain.

How many times do you remember talking to Jesus?

Twice. Although in some ways, in my mind, it seems like just once. Both times it seems like we were in the same place, the same mountainous setting. Our conversations were very similar, both were short, and he told me I had to go back both times. I have the impression it was two different conversations, but somehow it's hard to separate them.

In your memory, do all of these events seem to happen in order?

Not really. I mean, in my own mind, these are all separate memories not really tied together. I can't seem to put them in any sort of order…it's strange.

Tell me about returning to your body the first time—what do you remember?

I remember being in the hospital twice. The first time I guess I was in the emergency room or maybe pre-op. That's when they were touching my head. It seems like I had a fleeting glance of my body as I came back to it. I was small and I was on a bed or a stretcher, and there were people all around me doing things. They were all over me, trying to hook things up and checking my body. I don't think they were operating yet, my impression is that they were prepping me. Then I recall feeling like they were touching my head. I could actually feel it, so I must have been back in my body then. That's a very strong memory.

Did you have a sensation of pain whenever you re-entered your body?

Yes and no. I could feel something like dull pain in my head, but it was more a sense that something was wrong. My head felt more like it was swollen and achy but without actual pain. It was odd.

At this point in the session, you said angels were touching you—what do you remember about that?

It happened when I was in the hospital the first time. There were always three angels around me but suddenly the room where I was just filled with angels, these same kind of beings. I don't know how they got there, they just instantly appeared. They began moving around me and touching me all over and I could FEEL it! It was gentle and warm and was somehow invigorating. Then they were gone. It just happened for a few seconds and then it was over.

What happened after that?

I think that's when I left my body again and returned to Heaven, traveling up the same tunnel. This time, when I got to the end, I was suddenly back in the same mountainous area with Jesus.

What did you feel when you left your body? Was death an agonizing or painful experience?

No, not to me…not at all. I mean, I might have been feeling pain because I was injured, but there wasn't any pain or trauma leaving my body. In some ways, I don't recall the moment of leaving. I was just in my body one second and out of it the next. The transition wasn't all that noticeable, really.

Did you notice a great change in yourself outside of your body?

Not so much. I still knew who I was and felt basically the same. I do remember that my mind and my senses were sharper and it seemed like I knew things without being told. It was like I had a spiritual perception that I didn't have in my body. For instance, I knew Jesus and the angels instantly. Sometimes, it seemed like I knew on the inside what Jesus was going to say to me as He was saying it. Like I was hearing it on the inside at the same time my ears were hearing it. It's hard to describe, actually. But your senses are much sharper and your mind works differently, but yet I was the same person.

So you remember two trips to Heaven of some length?

Yes, I think so. The first one I saw the sheep, the rainbow, and Jesus told me to go back. I think the second is when He put His hands out to me and told me I was healed. Then there seems to be a third very short trip but I don't remember any details, just the tunnel and seeing a light. It was real short. It's hard to explain really.

What about the second conversation with Jesus?

Again, it didn't last too long, but He told me that He had healed me and to go back to the earth. I remember asking Him, just once, when was He coming back to Earth. He said "in time" and that it "wasn't time" yet, and that it would "take time." That's what I remember.

Did Jesus give you any more details of His coming back to Earth?

There was no date or year mentioned, if that's what you mean. *(laughs)* And, really, He didn't volunteer the information. He told me He was coming back "in time" and "when the time was right" in response to my question. You see, I didn't want to be parted from Jesus, so when He told me I couldn't stay there with Him, I asked Him when He was coming for me. See? The question I asked was really about me. It was for my benefit. In other words, if I couldn't stay with Jesus in Heaven, I wanted to know when He could come to Earth to be with me. All I know is I wanted to be with Jesus ANYWHERE. It didn't matter to me—either in Heaven or on Earth. I guess I was just reacting like any five-year-old might when I learned I couldn't stay. But I had the impression when He spoke that it might not be long, maybe in my lifetime. But I don't think even Jesus knew exactly when it would be.

During hypnosis, you said Jesus held out His hands toward you and told you you were healed—can you describe what happened?

Well, it seemed like He was just a few feet away but taller than I was, and as He began to move His hands toward me, it seemed like He bent forward slightly. But I don't remember Him actually touching or embracing me. I might have been on my knees but I don't specifically remember. He held out His hands toward me and told me, "You are healed," and that I had to go back.

When He held His hands out to you, do you remember seeing the nail prints?

No, I can't say I saw any nail prints in his hands or wrists. But honestly, I don't think I would have noticed them. I was just so completely captivated by his presence and his face that I just didn't look that closely at His hands. I wasn't expecting Him to reach His hands toward me to begin with, and then He only had them extended for a couple of seconds. They were not lifted very high and were palms down, so I probably couldn't have seen the nail prints from that angle anyway. I wish I would have seen them, but no, I didn't. We hardly ever went to church when I was little, so I'm not sure I would have known to look for them anyway...not at that age.

After Jesus told you that you were healed, is that when He said He loved you?

It happened after He told me I had to go back to the earth again. He told me that I had to go back several times. I was instantly saddened, almost panicked, and I have the impression He said it in response to my sadness. Although, as I think about it now, I'm not sure if He said that or whether I just knew it inside. I remember an intense wave of divine love that just washed over me. I don't exactly remember if I just felt this tidal wave of love when He spoke the words or if I just felt it and knew from this intense feeling that He loved me. Either way, it was over-powering. I'll never forget it. It makes me want to cry when I think about. I almost think He wanted me to experience this love to help overcome my sense of utter sadness at having to leave Heaven. Like it was something I could hold on to back on Earth. I can still feel the love all around me.

Are there any other details about Jesus' appearance you can remember?

Even now, when I see Him in my memory I can see His face and His upper body but somehow the specific details I can't recall, because when you are in His presence His face and eyes just overwhelm you. It captures your attention so much you just don't notice or can't focus on the details. You just see

Him as a whole but not the parts. It's hard to explain unless you've seen Him but His presence just swallows you up and you are oblivious to the details of His person. And, frankly, in some ways, you don't care about the details. You're standing in the awesome presence of the Son of God and the physical aspects of Jesus become meaningless compared to His glory. You could just FEEL WHO HE WAS! At least that's the way it was for me. I know exactly what He looks like, but outside of general things, I couldn't describe his specific appearance— yet I'd know Him again in an instant if I saw Him. I know that sounds contradictory but that's how it was for me when I saw Him. He seemed normal size for a man and He didn't have a crown on His head—I do remember that. He didn't have to say or do anything at all for me to know who He was. He's just surrounded by this radiance that no one else possesses. It's infinitely more intense than the angels. All I can say is that you just long to stay in His presence…forever. You never want to leave…never.

How did Jesus leave? Did He turn and walk away?

No, He just vanished. One second I'm in front of Him and in the next instant He's gone and I'm heading back to my body. I don't know if I'm just not remembering it or whether things in the spirit world just happen that quickly.

Do you remember how it felt to leave and re-enter your body?

Not really. There were a few times it seems like I was over top of my body, sort of hovering over it, seeing it from above. And then I was suddenly back inside of it and feeling whatever I was experiencing at the time. But I don't really remember the transition.

What do you recall about seeing Aunt Pat?

I remember Pat was just sitting there, reading or doing something. She just suddenly appeared before my eyes. Then she saw me, got up, and came over to the bed. She asked me if I wanted a cookie and I said 'no.' I had the impression that this wasn't the first time I woke up from the coma, but sometime later because Pat didn't seem surprised when she looked at me. And I remember she looked young.

Do you remember the kind of cookie she offered you?

No, I don't. *(laughing)*

So Pat is about the last recollection you recall from the session?

Yeah, I think so. I woke up after seeing Pat and I was in this room. And, for a few seconds didn't know where I was. Then I saw you and remembered we were in Parkersburg.

Is there anything else you remember or saw that we haven't talked about?

Well, there was another time I remember being out of my body, and when I left I saw Mom and Dad.

You saw Mom and Dad? Tell me about it.

I just remember going up—I always went up—leaving my body, and as I did I got a glimpse of Mom and Dad looking at me through a window of glass. They were just standing there. I think Mom was crying and Dad had his arm around her. Like Pat, they were both very young-looking. I remember feeling very, very sad because I was leaving them and I didn't want to go. It seemed like I was gone just a second, and when I came back to my body they were gone.

When you saw Mom and Dad, were there angels around you then?

Yes. Every single time I left my body, I could see them around me...always.

This episode must have occurred in the ICU after the operation.

I suppose that's true. I guess it had to be then, but seeing Mom and Dad is all I really remember of that episode. It's just a very brief but very clear memory. I also seem to have a faint recollection of seeing my body in the bed as I was going up or coming back, but just for a split second.

That would mean that you actually died — or left your body — four times, three times in pre-op, and another time in the ICU. Right?

Yeah, I guess that's true. In some ways, like I said, I can't piece it all together. These memories are all separate events but I can't recall the order they happened. The whole experience is sort of chopped up into separate pieces, some in my body and some out of my body. Maybe that's why they seem so disconnected from each other in my mind. I wish it were different, but that's the way it is.

Well, since we know what happened in the hospital during this time, it's possible to take your individual recollections and see how they fit together, right?

Oh, yeah…I think so. I'm just saying from my point of view I can't put them together in any order.

To me, it seemed like you re-lived the whole experience, under hypnosis, straight from beginning to end. But it doesn't seem that way to you?

No. But now that I've heard the tape, I think you're probably right about the order of things.

How did you feel when you woke up from the hypnotic trance?

Kind of strange. I remember my head hurt. I felt like I'd been in a deep, deep sleep. I was worn out when I woke up...and a little hungry. *(laughs)*

Do you remember feeling scared at any time during the session?

No, I don't remember being scared. Not even when I saw the car. And, when I think of it now, nothing scares or bothers me particularly.

What was the best part of the whole experience?

Are you kidding me? That's easy—being with Jesus. I never wanted to leave. There's nothing to compare with it here on Earth. It's funny, I didn't want to leave Earth, and when I got to Heaven I didn't want to come back. I'd given anything to stay. I'd go back there in a heart-beat. Oh YES! I'd go today. And you would too if you had been there in Heaven with Jesus like I was. It's indescribable.

How do you feel today? Are you different?

Yes, I definitely feel different. I feel better in every way. It seems like my memory is better, I'm calmer, I'm sleeping better. There's somehow just a feeling of relaxed confidence I didn't have before. I'm more relaxed about life in general. Nothing seems to bother me or upset me like before...even at work. *(laughs)* It's all better...I feel a BIG difference. I feel more like a whole person now. I can't explain it exactly but I don't think you can have an experience like that and it not change you profoundly. I think seeing Jesus and being in His Presence would change anybody for the better. Maybe I still sense being surrounded by the angels and by God's love. I'm not sure I can ever explain to anyone else, but the hole in my life is gone. Jesus filled it in with Himself. I know God knows me, loves me, and cares for me in a way I didn't understand before. It's like everywhere I go, I see it—it's always before me in my mind. I just have a whole new perspective on life now. I'm a different person on the inside and I wouldn't trade it for anything.

Do you feel close or closer to God?

Definitely…yes. I can just feel Him in me and all around me. It's not like a dream, I'm actually feeling His Presence in my everyday life and it continues day by day. I never felt this way before—ever.

Would you say you have less or no fear of death now?

Yes. I feel like it's not something to fear or be scared of. I feel like I'm ready from this point on. A person may be fearful of what causes their death, but leaving the body is not something to fear itself. Before, I'm sure I was fearful of death like most people, but not now. When I went through it, it wasn't frightening…not to me. It's like anything you've been through once or twice, it usually takes the fear away when you know what to expect. Leaving the body is the same way. There's no fear now.

So, all things considered, this experience was a great blessing to you?

Oh yes…no doubt. I'd do it again in a heart-beat. In every way it helped me. It gave me answers to questions I'd had all my life. It's like it filled in a bare spot in my life that affected me in a way that I could never quite put into words. I feel like I know more about ME now and that in itself brings a peace of mind. As the days go by, it seems like more and more of my true personality is emerging. People I work with notice a difference. I just feel whole...more complete...and that makes me more relaxed and friendlier, I guess. It's like the accident shut down a part of my life and this experience has opened it back up. It's great.

How would you say this has changed you?

In one sense it's easy to answer—it's like I was running on three cylinders after the accident and now I'm running on all four. It's a HUGE difference...to me anyway. It's like my true personality was lost and now it's emerging after being shut-up for forty years. It's like a miracle. One miracle saved my life, and forty years later another miracle has restored me and made me fully whole again. One miracle was physical, the other was spiritual. The circle of my life is complete now and I feel closer to God. What more could anyone possibly ask for? He's everything...

I am the resurrection, and the life;
he that believeth in me, though he were dead,
yet shall he live. And whosoever liveth and believeth
on me shall never die.
—John 11:25-26 (KJV)

Epilogue

OVER FOUR DECADES HAVE come and gone since that fateful day in February of 1970. My hometown of Ashland has certainly seen its share of changes—fewer people, fewer schools, a new bridge, a new mall, and of course, a Wal-Mart. Here, as elsewhere, the only constant is change itself.

Nestled along the banks of the Ohio River on the northeastern-most corner of Kentucky, Ashland has long been known for its coal, steel, and oil industries. But here, as with most towns in the Ohio Valley, the slow national decline in manufacturing has been more keenly felt, with Ashland losing almost one third of its population in recent decades. The town is presently inhabited by 22,000 hardy but aging souls, about 10,000 less than in its heyday a mere generation ago.

But all is not gloom. Despite its economic challenges, Ashland is still a very fine community in which to live and raise a family—with an abundance of excellent schools, a low crime rate, and a renewed sense of historic and civic pride.

Besides its long-held manufacturing reputation, the

town is also well-known for its high school sports program and for country music. In Ashland, we can lay claim to Major League pitcher Brandon Webb, the 2006 National League Cy Young Award Winner, and Grammy-winning Country Music stars The Judds, Naomi and Wynonna. Thankfully, they lay claim to us as well.

Aftermath

Today, the only physical remnants of the accident are the two "good-luck" pennies my Mom still keeps, tenderly preserved, a few hospital documents, and a single, yellowed, out-of-focus picture of the jagged scar on Billy's head taken several weeks after he came home. The memories of those awful days, like the scar on my left leg, have slowly and mercifully faded with the passage of time.

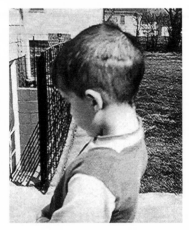

Billy's Surgical Scar (April, 1970)

But beyond the memories and those few keepsakes, the accident did have one profound and unexpected impact that remains to this day. Coming face-to-face with the supernatural power of God was such an eye-opening experience that it prompted a slow spiritual awakening, first in my father, and eventually spreading, one-by-one, to the entire family. Today, each family member is a born-again Believer with a vibrant and active faith—the one true and enduring legacy of the accident.

A father with four children, Bill now lives in Worthington, Kentucky, a scant ten miles down the river from his hometown. Sadly, my father passed away in 1983, never living to see the fine man his youngest son has become. My mother, enduring more than her share of health issues, moved from Ashland in 2003 and now lives with my sister Kathy in Richmond, Kentucky. Like most modern families, we are somewhat scattered—although four of my five siblings still live in Kentucky. My older sister Diana lives in Lexington and Bob is in Bowling Green, while John, the only Anderson living out-of-state now, resides in West Chester, Ohio.

Dr. Thomas Holbrook, Billy's gifted surgeon who pioneered neuroscience in Huntington, continued to serve the area for many years following Billy's surgery in 1970. When he retired in 1987, after 38 years of practice, he was nationally-renowned as an expert in the field of neuroscience. Ironically, Dr. Holbrook himself was diagnosed with a neurological condition, Parkinson's disease, later in life, and died in 2004 at the age of 86.

**The Anderson Siblings (1997). Clockwise from upper left:
Bob, Diana, Bill, John, Kathy, and Jim**

What of yours truly? Well, I still live on Monroe Street,
just one block from my old house and the scene of the accident.
The only one of the six children of Jim and Dorothy Anderson
to remain in Ashland, I've never felt the urge to leave. In fact,
except for college and my early married days, I have lived for
40 of my 52 years on the very same block of Monroe Street. It
just feels like home to me.

Though I've passed through the intersection of Monroe
and Kansas Streets countless times in the past 40 years, I
rarely think of the awful accident that occurred there. Even
now, when it is discussed in family circles, there is no hint

of trauma in the voices of Mom or my brothers and sisters. Instead of reliving the sorrow, we talk of the healing; instead of recalling the pain, we remember the triumph. This one incident, more than any other in my life, taught me first-hand that one of my Grandmother Anderson's favorite sayings is indeed true—"Things you cry about today, you'll laugh about tomorrow."

Signs of the Time

Like all streets in all towns, Monroe Street has seen its share of change in the last forty years. Most of the fine neighbors I knew from my youth have moved away or, regrettably, passed away. But there has been one singularly delightful change— Monroe Street has no shortage of stop signs now, four on every corner—the result of our accident so many years ago. Monroe still sees its share of traffic, especially during school hours, but it's nowhere near the drag-strip it used to be.

Most of our new neighbors pass by those stop signs without a single thought. But I never do. No matter how hurried I am, I make sure to stop at every corner. When I sit on my front porch in the evenings, I sometimes find myself staring at those bright red signs and remembering the awful price that was paid to put them in place—all the while conscious of a deeper significance.

You see, those aren't just stop signs to me, they are also signs of another kind. They don't just remind me of the past, they also point to the future. Each and every one is a gentle reminder of the fragile nature of life and the mercy and wonder of a miracle-working God. But most of all, those stop signs remind me of a five-year-old boy's spine-tingling prophecy—that God is true to His Word and that Jesus Christ, His Son, is coming soon...very soon.

And, behold, I come quickly; and my reward is with me,
to give every man according as his work shall be.
I am Alpha and Omega, the beginning and the end,
the first and the last.
—Revelation 22:12-13 (KJV)

If you found *I Saw God* to be a blessing, we would love to hear from you. Please visit **www.ISawGodBooks.com** and continue your experience.

- Read more about the upcoming *I Saw God* Book Series and submit your own story for consideration.
- Sign up to receive our monthly newsletter.
- Register to receive audio interviews with people who have had extraordinary Near-Death Experiences.
- Participate in our survey on life-after-death beliefs
- Communicate with the author.
- Register for a FREE copy of the first book in the *I Saw God* Book Series. Ten names will be randomly selected to receive a free copy. You could be one—register today!
- Purchase an e-book at a fraction of the retail price.
- Share your own thoughts and insights about *I Saw God* and read what others are saying on the *Forum* page.
- And much more…

For information on having the author speak to your church, organization, or group, please send an inquiry to isawgodbooks@gmail.com or write:

Anderson Communications Inc.
2760 Monroe Street, Suite 201
Ashland, KY 41102

Afterword

A WISE FRIEND ONCE told me that God doesn't waste miracles—He always uses them as seeds to grow the fruit of salvation. If God has spoken to your heart as you read this story and you have come to see your own personal need to become a Christian, I invite you to pray the following prayer and make Jesus the Lord of your life and receive God's free gift of eternal life. In simple child-like faith, say from your heart:

Heavenly Father, I come to You in the Name of Jesus, Your only begotten Son. Your Word says that "whosoever shall call on the name of the Lord shall be saved." As I call on Your name now, I know that you will save me. I humbly acknowledge that I am a sinner and I repent for my past life. I choose to turn from sin, and will live for You from this time onward.

Your Word says that "If I will confess with my mouth the Lord Jesus, and believe in my heart that God raised Him from the dead, I will be saved." Therefore, I believe and acknowledge that Jesus is Your Son, that He died for my sins, and rose from the dead for my justification according to the Scriptures; and I confess that Jesus is my Lord and Savior. Today, I accept your free gift of mercy, forgiveness, and eternal life through Jesus Christ and declare that I am now saved by faith. Thank you, Father, for hearing my prayer and being true to Your Word.

I pray this all in the name of Jesus. Amen.

Congratulations! If you prayed that prayer from your heart with faith and sincerity, you are now a born-again Christian, a child of the Living God. The following are a few specific suggestions to get you started on your Christian journey of faith:

- Find a Bible translation that you feel comfortable with and spend time with God each day reading His Word, primarily the New Testament, and praying.
- Share your new-found faith with someone else—friends, relatives, and co-workers, telling them what God has done for you.
- Begin to visit local churches, asking God to guide you to a Bible-believing, Spirit-led Church. Remember, the largest church, the most convenient church, or the church with the most friends is not always the best church for you.
- Once you find a Church home, get baptized in water and

then baptized in the Holy Ghost. The baptism in the Holy Ghost is an experience that will empower you to live the Christian life and be the effective witness that God wants you to be.

- Develop relationships with other believers in your new church and in your neighborhood and get involved in church activities, using your individual talents and abilities to further the Kingdom of God.

If this book has been instrumental in your decision to follow Christ, or has been a source of comfort and inspiration in your Christian walk, we would love to hear from you. Please feel free to share your experience with us at isawgodbooks@gmail.com. All communication from readers is kept strictly confidential.

Now the God of peace,
that brought again from the dead our Lord Jesus,
that great shepherd of the sheep,
through the blood of the everlasting covenant;
make you perfect in every good work to do his will,
working in you that which is well-pleasing in his sight,
through Jesus Christ, to whom by glory forever and ever.
Amen.
—Hebrews 13:20-21 (KJV)

A Special Note from the Author

A PORTION OF THE proceeds of this book will go toward my favorite ministry—The JESUS Film Project.® The most translated, viewed, and distributed film in history, the *JESUS* film is a powerful tool for global evangelism because of its accurate portrayal of the gospel. The classic edition alone has been translated into more than 1,100 languages and is used by hundreds of mission organizations and church-planting movements. Whatever the culture, people respond when hearing Jesus speak their "heart" language.

The Reverend Billy Graham said, **We thank God for the many people whose lives have been transformed as a result of seeing the JESUS film as it has been shown around the world over the past 25 years**.

Pastor Rick Warren, author of *The Purpose-Driven Life*, said, **The JESUS film is the most effective evangelistic tool ever invented...**

Jerry Rankin, President of International Mission Board, said, *Whether in closed countries, illiterate cultures, or in places of open harvest, the graphic portrayal in the JESUS film has radically accelerated the potential for fulfilling the Great Commission.*

Please visit www.jesusfilm.org to find out how you can get involved by going on a short-term JESUS Film mission trip, obtain a copy of *JESUS* or its derivatives (which include *Magdalena: Released From Shame, Magdalena: Through Her Eyes,* and *The Story of Jesus for Children*), view the film online in more than 800 languages, or give to the ministry of The JESUS Film Project. You may also call (800) 387-4040.

Thank you!

About The Author

JIM ANDERSON WAS BORN and raised in Ashland, KY. He graduated from Paul G. Blazer High School and then earned a Bachelor of Science degree in Mechanical Engineering from the University of Kentucky. He has spent most of his professional career as a Project Manager and Engineering Consultant to AK Steel in Ashland. He is also a freelance writer, contributing many articles and editorials to *The Christian Perspective,* a quarterly journal on contemporary issues.

Jim is also the author and editor of a unique Bible study-aid, *The COMPLEAT Gospel of Jesus.* To create this fascinating book, Jim used sophisticated computer technology to systematically dissect, analyze, and seamlessly blend the four KJV Gospels in a single spectacular story that presents every recorded event in the life and ministry of Jesus Christ in precise chronological order and includes every element of detail that can be gleaned from the original Gospels. The result of this synthesis is a fully-integrated reference work on the life of Jesus so thoroughly complete and refreshingly different that you might think you're reading the Gospel story for the first time.

Jim is also an award-winning songwriter and portrait artist, and the owner of Anderson Art Studios. He continues to live with his family in Ashland. He is married to the former Catherine Ann Thompson and they have two sons, Matthew (Jamie) and David, and one grandson, John Carter.